6 PRINCIPLES
for Achieving
PERSONAL
BALANCE

James B. Lewis, LCSW, CSAT

ATTENTION Organizations and businesses:

This book is available at quantity discounts on bulk purchases
for educational, business, or sales promotion use.

For further information,
please contact Guiding Path by e-mail at: jimlewis@guidingpath.biz

Table of Contents

Acknowledgments

Scores of people; friends, professional associates, and especially clients have contributed significantly to the outcome of this workbook. I owe a debt of gratitude to so many people for their ideas and feedback.

I especially want to thank Darla Isackson who did the copy editing and Lissel Dalton for their patience and tireless feedback (and red notes in my manuscript). They have been stalwarts for me and are responsible for helping put many of my ideas into words, diagrams and worksheets. I also extend my gratitude to Linda Gundry and Korrin Ebira who reviewed my manuscript and gave me wonderful, constructive feedback.

I give my thanks to Rod Jeppsen for his assistance with Chapter Six, along with the many other suggestions that have been insightful and given me direction. I am also grateful to the innumerable student interns whom I have supervised, who have applied the principles from the book and given invaluable feedback and observations.

Over thirty six years as a professional counselor I have had the opportunity and privilege to share ideas with many business associates who have given feedback and helpful suggestions and to them I say a big thank you.

To my family, I think they are giving a big sigh of relief as this book has been in the making for many years. A big thanks to them for their patience and support.

SIX PRINCIPLES FOR ACHIEVING PERSONAL BALANCE

To those of you who might be new readers, I thank you and wish you well as you journey through the six principles which, has truly been a labor of love for me.

Thanks

James B. Lewis, LCSW, CSAT

Preface

In 1985 I was browsing through the self-help section of a bookstore, when I picked up a book titled, *Traits of a Healthy Family*, by Delores Curran. On the back cover, I read about a survey Curran had conducted. Five hundred survey responses from professional counselors were summarized as a list of fifteen qualities they all believed healthy families had in common. Communication and listening were on the top of everyone's list. An affirming and supportive environment was second. Based on my experience as a counselor and father, this approach rang true to me, so I opened the book.

In the preface, Curran talked about getting away from a "pathology model" (concentrating on what is wrong instead of what is working). Her approach encourages us to focus upon our family's health by becoming aware of the traits commonly found in healthy families. I prefer to call the major guidelines "principles" rather than traits. Guiding principles, applicable to every situation, can give families what they need to move closer to the health/wellness idea Curran presents.

I have expanded on those principles to make them easier to apply, and have chosen to present the principles of balance in relationships in a series of three books which go in to more detail about healthy relationships. The books focus separately on: (1) Personal Balance, (2) Marital Unity, and (3) Peace and Harmony within the Family. In book one: *Six Principles for Achieving Personal Balance*, you will learn six important principles of personal balance, how balance affects all other relationships, and how to establish it in your life. In book two: *Six Principles for Achieving Marital Unity* you will learn six principles for developing balance and unity in your marital relationship. Book three: *Six Principles for Achieving Family Harmony* is about the important relationships in your family and how to establish peace and harmony within these relationships.

Few things are more important than the relationships ou have with your family. These relationships have a profound influence for positive or negative on your daily life. Some relationships work very well, while others can be very destructive. Learning and applying the principles described in this book will help you balance *all* the important relationships in your life. Learning the Six Principles for Achieving Personal Balance is crucial for individuals and families to survive the pressures placed on them in today's world.

Over the years, I have developed handouts, worksheets, questionnaires, etc. for my clients, and have spent a great deal of time refining them I have received feedback regarding these materials from clients, friends, and other professionals. Remarks such as, "I wish I had been taught these principles ten years ago," "These principles have changed my life for the better," and "I have a sense of balance in my life now that I have never experienced before," are common remarks. Over the last ten years, as I started putting these principles into a workbook format, I have seen the benefit of their application in individual and couples' lives and wish to extend these benefits to you, the reader.

Introduction
to the Six Principles
for Achieving Personal Balance

Years ago it became clear to me that when my clients did six specific things, they would get through their problems quicker and easier. Consequently, I developed the Six Principles for Achieving Personal Balance. I also found that the six principles became even more powerful as agents for positive change when people followed three specific guidelines:

1. Learn
  a. Learn everything you can about whatever problem you are working on.
  b. Learn about every tool that would be helpful, and study how to use them.

2. Believe
  a. Develop hope, self-confidence, and faith that the tools you have learned will help you in overcoming whatever problem you are working on.
  b. Believing that every problem has buried within itself an inherent good brings an enormous amount of hopefulness and gives a whole new outlook on the challenges in your life.

3. Do

a. Think of the word DONE. The first part of <u>do</u>ne is <u>do</u>. You have to do in order to be done.

b. However, your "doing," in order to be effective and beneficial, must be focused on the specific tools and behaviors you have learned and have come to believe in.

You will find that utilizing these three fundamental guidelines will enhance the effectiveness of the six principles.

Applying the fundamental guidelines to the Six Principles for Achieving Personal Balance will enrich your life because they help bring order and direction to what you think and do. Personal balance is always the place to start; if your personal life is out of balance, it is likely your relationships with the important people in your life will also be out of balance.

My goal for the six principles is to give you practical how-to skills that you can learn easily and use immediately. Each concept taught is followed by worksheets to help you apply and reinforce what you have learned. The worksheets can be used over and over again because they are based upon principles of relationships; while needs may change as you go through life, the principles of relationships will not.

I find that I learn so much from those who use the six principles, and they have enriched my own life tremendously. I would like to invite you to make comments and suggestions as you read the six principles. You can do so by emailing me at: jimlewis@guidingpath.biz.

1

Personal Balance

Have you heard yourself saying any of the following lately? "I don't have time for *me* anymore." "I think I'm having an identity crisis." "I'm so tired all the time." "I don't remember the last time I did something just for me." "Fun, what is that?"

You're not alone! The following comments are also common: "I'm just too busy to take time for a vacation this year." "I haven't been on a date with my spouse for months." "I wish we could find time to talk."

If you have caught yourself saying things like the above, you are among a large and growing number of individuals, couples, and families. You may be suffering from a problem called *Out of Balance Syndrome* (OBS). If you have OBS, you do and say things that are not healthy for the relationship you have with yourself and with others. OBS will be discussed in detail in this and following chapters.

Is Your Life Balanced?

Achieving personal balance is not something we attain once and then never have to work on again. It is an ongoing dynamic process based on such things as your age, life circumstances, and needs at the time. Successful business owners want to balance their personal life with their work. Employees want to find balance between their family life and their job responsibilities. Knowing how to achieve personal balance between all the competing influences and demands of external factors and other relationships is crucial to having peace and wellness in your life.

Maintaining balance is one of the major challenges of life. Balance is ever-changing and dynamic and can seem elusive. When you are out of balance you can become distressed and discouraged.

Learning and applying the Six Principles for Achieving Personal Balance described in this book will help you develop and maintain a healthier, more contented life in spite of the external chaos going on around you.

Take for example the challenge of finding balance between your physical self and your emotional self. These two factors are so closely associated and dependent on each other, you cannot change one without having an effect, positively or negatively, upon the other system. For example, learning to slow your breathing to approximately twenty times per minute will help you cope better with stress because that is the balance your system likes. In this next section we will discuss the challenge of meeting needs in healthy, balanced ways.

Needs, the Role They Play in Your Life, and How to Balance Them

A "need" is something you perceive to be necessary, something you feel you must have or do. A need indicates a void you want to fill. You may have a physical need to fill your stomach because you are hungry, or an emotional need to have someone to talk to because you are lonely.

One of the best known theorists regarding needs is Abraham Maslow, who developed the "Hierarchy of Needs" theory, in which he lists five levels of ascending needs: (1) physiological needs, (2) safety and security needs, (3) love and belonging needs, (4) esteem needs, and (5) the need to self-actualize. He believed that once you meet the need to survive (air, water, food, minerals, vitamins, etc.) you can then attend to the need for safety (stability in life, protection, to have structure in one's life, a home, to live in a safe neighborhood, etc.).

Once the physiological and safety needs are filled, you may begin to feel the need for connection with others (friends, companion, children, a sense of community, etc.). Sometimes filling the need for connection is a challenge because a person has poor social skills or is shy. If you isolate yourself you cannot meet this need in healthy ways. Learning to connect with others, even though it might be hard, is a key to success in the next stages of need as defined by Maslow. The next level, esteem is broken into two sub-levels. The lower level need is associated with status, recognition, reputation and dignity; it relates to outward things--how you believe others see you. The higher need relates to how you feel about yourself--the need for self-respect, self-confidence, competence, self-mastery, independence.

When your survival is threatened or when you are under stressful conditions, Maslow believes you regress to a lower level in the hierarchy. For example, if you have just been told a reduction in the workforce means you will be losing your job, you may not have the energy to think about anything but how you are going to make the next mortgage payment. Even if you had been feeling secure and your esteem was strong, because your security has been taken away, you may regress to wondering how you are going to survive.

The top level of the hierarchy is self-actualization. If you want to be truly self-actualizing, you must first take care of needs lower on the hierarchy, such as finding a job. Being self-actualized is the drive to "be the best that you can be." It takes a great deal of healthy energy to become the true "you." For example if you are without food, you will be focused on getting some, if you are feeling unsafe, you will be on your guard; all of which takes time and energy away from being able to self-actualize. Only when lower needs are met are you able to fully devote yourself to fulfilling the higher needs necessary to become self-actualized.

Balancing Needs

It takes *balance* to meet your needs in healthy ways. For example, the need to eat is healthy and necessary for survival. However, going beyond the necessity to survive by eating too much is unhealthy and causes you to be "out of balance" physically.

OBS (Out of Balance Syndrome) can also happen when you are trying to meet your emotional needs. For example, if you were to focus all your time and attention on only one friend, at the exclusion of others, that friend might eventually feel smothered and start avoiding you. Over time this pattern could cause you to lose a lot of friends and create a sense of loneliness, as well as cause you to be "out of balance" emotionally.

Any time you OVERemphasize an area of need at the expense of other needs (example: overemphasis of individual needs while minimizing marital needs), you will suffer from OBS. Emotional symptoms of OBS include: loneliness, shame, being cross and irritable, low self-esteem, addictive behaviors, and depressed feelings. Physical symptoms of OBS include being tired and sleepy most of the day, crying excessively, low energy, and feeling stress or anxiety.

The Out of Balance Syndrome can be corrected by learning to find balance between your needs as an individual and the needs and demands of all your other relationships. This concept is depicted in the following diagram (Fig. 1.1):

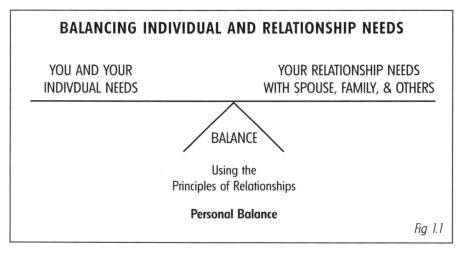

BALANCING INDIVIDUAL AND RELATIONSHIP NEEDS

YOU AND YOUR
INDIVDUAL NEEDS

YOUR RELATIONSHIP NEEDS
WITH SPOUSE, FAMILY, & OTHERS

BALANCE

Using the
Principles of Relationships

Personal Balance

Fig 1.1

The diagram (Fig. 1.2) below will be a brief introduction to three developmental stages of relationships. The chart shows that as you grow and develop, your relationship needs grow and get more complicated and demanding as well, especially with regards to your own needs and the demands of relationships with others. This diagram is explained in detail on the following pages (pages 4-15).

How Individual Needs Develop During the Growing Up Process (Fig. 1.2 "a – Individual")

Let's begin by comparing your individual needs to a cup of water. Keep in mind that you want your "cup" to be as full as possible. When you are growing up, at least initially, you try to get most of your physical and emotional needs met by your parents or guardians. By observing how your parents and siblings fill their cups, and what part of their cups they give to you, you begin to form a positive or negative idea of who you are. There are many different types of parental "cups," for example, vacant cups, empty cups, abusive cups, neglectful cups, inconsistent cups, and, of course, healthy cups. When you drink from a healthy parental cup, you come away feeling refreshed, empowered, encouraged, loved, and accepted for who you are

However, If you go to your parent(s) in an effort to fill a need by drawing from their "cup," and come away with a black eye or bloody nose (abusive cup), or you get nothing (empty cup), you can be devastated! If this happens frequently, you may begin thinking that *maybe* you are not lovable, capable, or wanted. This can set the stage for OBS and faulty core beliefs (see below).

If the parental cup you drink from is inconsistent or neglectful, you will tend to feel confused and lonely, and will likely see the world as a place that cannot be trusted. Your judgment can become impaired, making it easier to fall prey to the many pitfalls in the world; you may begin making unwise choices.

Over time, when this pattern continues, you begin asking yourself unpleasant and disturbing questions about your character (core). "Why do I get nothing when I drink from my father/mother's cup?" "Is there something wrong with me?" Eventually the ultimate faulty core belief begins to develop, "Maybe I am not worthy of getting anything, maybe I am *just a bad, unworthy person!*" Faulty core beliefs such as these always lead to OBS (saying and doing things that aren't healthy for the relationship you have with yourself and others).

Faulty Core Beliefs

A core belief is a very strong conviction you have about yourself. These beliefs affect how you think and behave, and thus have an impact on the relationship you have with yourself and others in a positive or negative way. Once established, a core belief is difficult but *not* impossible to change. An example of a healthy core belief might be "I am basically a good person."

Faulty core beliefs (FCB) begin developing early in life and are usually set in place by the teenage years. Examples of faulty core beliefs might be, "I am basically a bad, unworthy person," or, "I am such a loser." For a specific example of how core beliefs develop, let's consider Alex:

All during his growing up years, whenever Alex would ask for his father's approval, he would get a response such as: "You will have to do it over because you didn't do it right," or "Alex, when are you ever going to learn to do this right"? Alex was a 4.0 student through high school; his first semester in college he was on the Dean's honor roll. But as much as he tried, he could never get his father to acknowledge the good he did in his life.

On one occasion, his father asked him to paint the front door. Alex spent hours painstakingly painting every nook and cranny and was so proud of what he had done. Unfortunately, when his father inspected it all he saw and commented on was a barely visible and tiny spot that Alex had missed. Alex's father was probably passing on faulty core beliefs he learned from his father; for example, "unless you do something perfectly it has little or no value." Alex came to believe that the only way to gain his father's love was to be perfect all the time—a clearly impossible condition.

Some sons would have just said "Oh well, I don't need Dad's approval; I know I'm a good person in spite of the fact he never recognizes the good job I do." However, Alex had a tender nature, and took to heart his father's negative attitude. He came to believe he was doomed to be an inadequate person in spite of the enormous talents he was gifted with. Alex believed he couldn't do anything well; consequently, his core belief became: "I am inadequate and will never measure up to my father's expectations."

When you have consistent negative experiences in life and conclude that something is seriously wrong with you as a person, a mechanism called the belief filter is put in place. Every word that is said to you and every experience from then on passes through that belief filter. Only those that validate the belief that you are **not** a person of worth are let in—the rest you ignore or distort. Since your experiences seem to continually validate your negative belief, you become more and more convinced that it is true. The following diagrams (Fig. 1.3 and 1.4) describe this phenomenon. (Strategies for stopping and correcting faulty core beliefs will be taught in chapters six and nine.) Who you believe you are, determines how you act and react. Your core beliefs form the context out of which all else evolves. Let's see how this applies to your belief filter.

Figure 1.3 shows the basic faulty core belief concept and figure 1.4 uses an example to show how the concept applies.

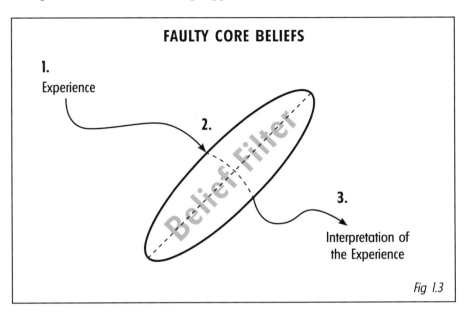

FAULTY CORE BELIEFS

1.
Experience

2.

Belief Filter

3.
Interpretation of
the Experience

Fig 1.3

Thought or Behavior

Let's walk through Figure 1.4 first, keeping in mind figure 1.3 while we do so. If, for example your parent was rejecting like Alex's father, and the rejection was a consistent experience, you were likely to wonder about and doubt your worth as a person.

Example: "Maybe I'm not worth very much."

This thought passes through the Belief Filter...

Interpretation of the Thought or Behavior

Over time, the rejection by Alex's father had been so consistent that he started to believe he was of very little worth.

Example: "I am worthless!"

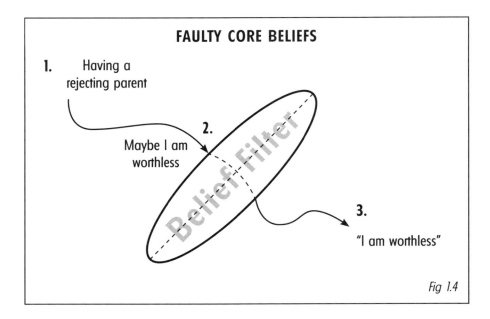

FAULTY CORE BELIEFS

1. Having a rejecting parent

2. Maybe I am worthless

Belief Filter

3. "I am worthless"

Fig 1.4

The more Alex dwelt on the possibility that he might be worthless, the more he came to believe it and consequently play it out in his life by putting himself down and doubting he could do anything right.

Typical core beliefs:

- If I don't please people, they may choose to reject, criticize, or not like me.
- I must be close to perfect in everything I do or I will be rejected.
- I must rely on others.
- I have a feeling that the past determines the present.
- I can't share my feelings.
- I can't become anything I believe is above me.
- I must be successful in everything I do.
- I must have others approval for everything I do or I'm a failure.

Positive affirmations can make a big difference in your core beliefs:

- I appreciate my talents and abilities.
- I depend on myself for getting my needs met.
- I am basically a good person.

- I would never purposely hurt anyone.
- I deserve to be respected.
- I make mistakes, but that doesn't define who I am.
- It's okay for me to learn at my own pace.
- It's okay for me to establish and keep boundaries with others.

Each of the *Six Principles for Achieving Personal Balance* will address how to change faulty core beliefs and help you develop new ways of thinking and behaving. In chapter nine, you will see how the six principles apply in repairing FCB's.

Everyone has been disappointed at one point or another because their needs were not met; that is a part of life. The *Faulty Core Belief Worksheet*, below, will help you identify when unmet needs have become a pattern in your life, and the impact that has had on you.

FAULTY CORE BELIEFS WORKSHEET

Once you have taken on and accepted a faulty core belief it is difficult to break away from and change how you think and how you behave, but it is possible and necessary. A lot of effort on your part will be required in order to achieve personal balance.

Identify an experience with a parent or significant other in which a need was not met.

Example: *My father didn't come to any of my athletic events in high school.*

_____

_____

Process that experience through the belief filter, listing the process below.

Thought or behavior
Ex: *It must not have been very important to him.*

_____

_____

_____

Interpretation of thought or behavior
Ex: *I'm not important to him.*

_____

_____

_____

How did you interpret this experience? (i.e. what are your thoughts, feelings, etc.) Was your interpretation negative or positive?

_____

_____

_____

_____

_____

Is your interpretation a *core belief* that you have held for a long time? Describe how and when you first became aware of this.

_____

_____

_____

_____

If your interpretation was negative, how has it affected your behavior?

_____

_____

_____

_____

The six principles for achieving personal balance can help you change faulty core beliefs. In chapter nine you will find a worksheet and more information on how you can evaluate the faulty core belief(s) you have identified here, and then apply the six principles as change agents to repair you faulty core beliefs.

Remember that you want your "cup" to be as full as possible in healthy, hopeful ways. Let's say, for example, that two or three of your needs are not being met; you may not know what your needs are, or you may be ignoring them or putting them off until your children grow up. If this is the case, you will, at some point suffer from OBS. You run the risk of meeting your needs (filling your cup) in unhealthy ways in an effort to fill the void.

Identifying your individual needs and establishing a plan to consistently fill them in healthy ways, is a significant part of life. Examples of individual needs might be time to think and plan; to develop interests, talents, hobbies, a healthy body, high self-esteem, to have personal space, to feel productive, educated, creative, and spiritual. Another important need is the need to *feel* or to *allow yourself to feel*.

The key to success in developing *healthy core beliefs* is learning to identify and label thoughts as they come through the belief filter, to reinforce the positive ones, and to challenge the negative ones immediately. You will learn more about this in the chapters that follow. Common thinking errors:

1. "If I think it, then I am what I thought."

2. "I thought it, so my thought *must* be my reality."

Many tools will be introduced in this book, *Six Principles for Achieving Personal Balance*, which will help you identify and conquer the harmful effects of faulty core beliefs. The following worksheet will help you identify specific individual needs and set goals to meet those needs.

INDIVIDUAL NEEDS WORK SHEET

In order to meet your needs in healthy ways, you must first *identify* your needs. Once you identify, you can develop a program to support your healthy needs using this worksheet.

Needs: those things you feel are necessary to survive physically, emotionally, and spiritually.

Using the form below, list one or two individual needs. Examples: to be more productive, to make time to develop talents and interests, to set aside time to study and meditate, to develop higher self-esteem (see Chapter Seven). You will notice there is space for only two supporting activities. You will be more successful if you list only two for each need you want to work on. Long lists of activities may overwhelm you and set you up for failure. List one physical need and one emotional need to begin with. When you are consistent in following through with your plan to meet those two needs, add another need to your worksheet.

Example:

Need   **Supporting activities**

To have higher self-esteem.   a. *Do one activity a month just for fun.*

                                                      b. *Read a book on self-esteem.*

I plan to start my supporting activities on   *10/12/06*
                                                                              date

---

Need   **Supporting activities**

                                                      a.

                                                      b.

I plan to start my supporting activities on   _____
                                                                              date

Need   **Supporting activities**

                                                      a.

                                                      b.

I plan to start my supporting activities on   _____
                                                                              date

The Needs of Your Marital/Significant Other Relationship

Going to Figure 1.2 (p.), which shows that as you grow and develop, your relationship needs grow and get more demanding. Following it up to "b" (couple) you will notice the diagram not only flows upward from individual needs, but also expands. This is to show that the need base has now expanded to include the needs of the marital/significant other relationship.

At times, this expansion of needs can present a dilemma because you are still an individual with all your own needs. The temptation will be to lose yourself in the relationship at the expense of your individual needs. The key is to find a healthy balance between the needs of the relationship and your individual

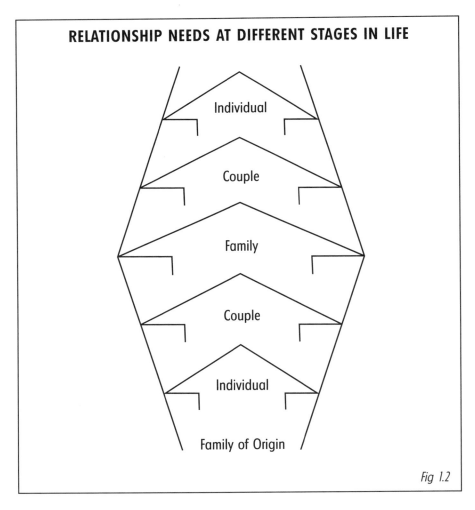

RELATIONSHIP NEEDS AT DIFFERENT STAGES IN LIFE

Individual

Couple

Family

Couple

Individual

Family of Origin

Fig 1.2

needs. Typical pitfalls that contribute to loss of self in the relationship are thoughts such as:

- It's selfish of me to think of myself and my needs.
- I'll do something for me later--maybe next year.
- It's my responsibility to make my spouse/significant other happy.
- It must be all my fault we are having problems.

In reality, unhappiness or lack of unity in the relationship almost always has multiple causes; it is never the total responsibility of one person or the other.

A very wise person said something like, "You cannot drink water from an empty bucket." Constantly giving and never receiving is unhealthy and out of balance for you, but also for the other person in the relationship. A healthy relationship requires that both give, receive, and serve each other. If the giving is all one way, you may develop feelings of resentment, loneliness, and feeling taken advantage of and taken for granted. The worksheet on the next page will help you identify specific relationship needs and help you set goals to meet those needs.

RELATIONSHIP NEEDS WORKSHEET

Needs are a vital part of everyone's life. Because there are personal needs and relationship needs, it is important to distinguish between the two. This worksheet focuses on the relationship needs you have with others. Begin by picking two needs. Examples of various types of relationship needs might be: companionship, trust and trustworthiness, understanding, approval/validation, acceptance and feeling that you belong, appreciation, appropriate touch, intimacy, communication, encouragement, etc.

As you identify needs, you can develop a program to fill them in healthy ways using this worksheet.

Example:

Need   **Supporting activities**

To be a person my spouse can trust   a. *Learn about the traits of people who can be trusted (in Chapter Three).*

                                                b. *When I say I'll be home to make sure I get there when I promised.*

I plan to start my supporting activities on   <u>*10/12/06*</u>
                                                         date

---

Need   **Supporting activities**

                                                a.

                                                b.

I plan to start my supporting activities on   _____
                                                         date

Need   **Supporting activities**

                                                a.

                                                b.

I plan to start my supporting activities on   _____
                                                         date

The Needs of Your Family Relationships and Their Individual Needs (Fig. 1.2 "c – Family")

Following Figure 1.2 (p. 11) up to "c" (family), you will notice this section takes up a proportionately larger part of the diagram. This is because you and your spouse spend such a large part of your life in this phase. You will also notice the diagram expands at first and then begins to narrow.

As children are born, the family expands in numbers and the need base expands. Later, children get married, go off to college, work, etc.; thus, the number at home full-time declines. Keep in mind that once children come into the home and you are a family, the need base expands. As you draw your individual and couple needs into the family stage, you might catch yourself saying something like, "Wow, my family has lots of needs too!" You have needs, your spouse has needs, and your children have needs. In addition, there are the needs of your marital and family relationships. Depending on how well your needs have been met to this point you will have more or less to give to family relationships in this stage. OBS in your marital/significant other relationship, will have a significant negative impact on the quality of your family relationships.

Remember that your children will be observing you to get an idea of how needs are met. You cannot overlook the enormous and profound influence of parents and siblings on each individual. Go back to Figure 1.2. You will notice a circle around Individual "a" titled "family of origin."

Whether you grew up in a single-parent family, or with both parents, an adopted family, a family with grandparents, aunts and uncles, a foster family, as an only child or with eight siblings, your family of origin has a big impact on you. Relationship needs at different stages in life will be discussed in more detail in *Book Three, Six Principles for Achieving Peace and Harmony in Family Relationships.*

The worksheet on the following page will help you identify a balanced approach to meeting the needs of all the important relationships in your life.

HEALTHY NEEDS PLANNING WORKSHEET

This worksheet helps encourage balance between the major relationships in life because, like many, you may tend to overemphasize one need at the expense of the other needs in your life.

Self   List two things you are willing to commit to do just for you. Spouses, children, friends, and others should not be included. This should be two specific, well-defined activities that will help boost how you feel about yourself. Then list two supporting activities for each:

Example:

1. *Start taking better care of my physical self.*

   a. *Walk two nights a week.*

   b. *Workout one night a week.*

1. _____

   a. _____

   b. _____

2. _____

   a. _____

   b. _____

Spouse   List two things you are willing to commit to do with your spouse. Children, relatives, friends, and others, should not be included. This should be planned together with the intent that the activities chosen will strengthen the marital relationship. Example: scheduling a date.

1. _____ planned with spouse _____
                                                    date(s)

2. _____ planned with spouse _____
                                                    date(s)

Family List one activity you are willing to organize and be responsible for carrying out with your family. List another activity that you will commit to do with each of your children one-on-one. An example of a family activity would be organizing a family picnic. An example of an individual activity with each child would be specifically setting aside time to help your child with his/her science project.

1. Family activity

_____

2. Individual activity with each child
a. _____
b. _____
c. _____

Others Decide on an activity you would like to do with a special friend and then take responsibility to carry it out. (A double date with friends or a family picnic with another family are examples that would meet this need.)

1. _____

* You will be more likely to follow through if you have someone to report to about activities you have committed to do.

Although Chapter One covers many concepts, you will begin to see in the remaining chapters how the Six Principles for Achieving Personal Balance tie together like strands of a very strong and durable rope. Learning everything you can about the principles of personal balance will help you develop a greater sense of self-confidence in conquering challenges in your life. It will also increase your belief that you can take control of yourself in ways that have a positive impact on those things that are important to you.

Control of your life begins by controlling the nature and quality of your thoughts. We will talk a lot about this concept of control in the following chapters. Change your thinking and you will *indeed*, change your life!

Notes and Insights

2

The Principles of Personal Balance:
An Overview

In chapter one, we discussed the importance of establishing personal balance, identifying needs and developing a plan to make sure your "cup" is being filled in healthy ways. When your cup is not being filled in healthy ways, you experience Out of Balance Syndrome (OBS), which results in unhealthy thoughts, words, and actions that damage all your important relationships. In this book you will learn more specific ways to develop individual balance and avoid OBS.

The remaining chapters discuss in greater detail the individual stage (refer to Fig. 1.2 "a", pg 11) and the six principles necessary for developing individual balance. These principles, when applied, will help you become more balanced and will free up more of your energy to give to other relationships.

Each chapter provides specific ideas and exercises to help you develop balance as an individual.

I was watching a documentary on China recently where people were carrying supplies on yokes across their shoulders. (Many people in China make their living transporting supplies in this fashion.) The documentary showed how carefully the people equalized the weight on both sides of the yoke because their livelihood depends on it. If the loads are not balanced, their backs can be thrown out or their spinal discs can wear unevenly. However, workers who are patient and careful about equalizing the weight, can last for years in this profession.

In a similar documentary about the people of Tibet, I watched villagers travel many miles to gather wood, carrying enormous loads on their backs. I wondered how they could accomplish such a feat, and learned that the villagers wove the branches into bundles that were equal in weight from side to side; the heavier the load, the more important the balance. They spent considerable time picking the right branches and then weaving them into the bundles in just the right way.

These experiences exemplify the importance of achieving and maintaining emotional, physical, social, and spiritual balance in life. Remember, it is important not to OVERemphasize any life-element, such as physical exercise, at the expense of the other important areas of your life. You will notice that as you begin mastering the six principles of personal balance you will experience a feeling of stability and control in your life. A brief summary of the six principles of personal balance follows.

Trust

It is natural to want to be trusted and to have friends you can trust. Learning to trust yourself is the root of healthy trust. The relationship you have with yourself has more effect on your relationships with others than any other variable. For example, if you develop a pattern in your life of keeping promises you make to yourself, you are more likely to keep promises you make to others. Of course, the opposite is true as well. If you take a casual approach to the promises you make to yourself, you are likely to take the same approach in your other relationships.

Trust is the foundation for all the principles of personal balance. We need to ask ourselves two major questions about trust: (1) Am I a person who can be trusted? and (2) What factors contribute to trusting relationships with others? Learning when to trust, how to trust, and when not to trust are essential tasks.

Boundaries in Relationships

Boundaries define how you distinguish yourself from others physically and emotionally—how you define your own accountability and let others have theirs. It is also protecting your right to make your own choices and keep yourself safe. Without boundaries you will not be able to develop healthy relationships. Some people will inevitably violate your boundaries. How do you know when a boundary has been violated and what you should do about it? This important question will be answered.

Knowing how to establish and maintain good boundaries will enhance your physical and emotional health. Good boundaries promote good relationships. Good boundaries begin with knowing yourself, knowing what you want and need. Start developing healthy boundaries by developing a clear plan. True friends respect your boundaries and are open and accepting when you tell them they have crossed a boundary with you.

Energy and Conflict Management

Few things are more frustrating in life than trying to control things (or people) you have little or no control over. Even when we know this principle we can easily find ourselves stuck in the controlling mode. Learning how to identify and manage things you can control, or have significant influence over, while letting go of things you can't control are critical skills to achieving personal and relationship balance. Many things compete for your attention (television, work, family, recreation, etc.), so it is critical to have a balanced plan for using your energy in order to accomplish what is most important and avoid wasting energy on futile efforts.

This chapter will teach you how to identify and manage your conflicts. Applying the principles can bring healthy energy back to you, establishing healthier balance in your every-day life.

Self-Control

In a day and age where affluence, self-gratification and pride are blatantly advertised as prized qualities/possessions, it is not easy to apply self-control.

Yet, self-control is critical to achieving personal balance and healthy relationships with others. Controlling your thoughts is a prime example. Identifying and labeling unwanted thoughts quickly, then purposefully choosing not to follow through with them is of prime importance. Five tools to accomplish this important task will be presented.

Self-Esteem

Healthy self-esteem is not to be confused with selfish love or the feeling that you are better than anyone else. It is not the drive to become perfect as opposed to working on improving your life to find balance. (Perfectionism always leads to OBS.)

Self-esteem is important because you must first have a healthy love for self before you can truly love others. It is essential to identify and label the enemies of strong, healthy self-esteem, then develop beneficial strategies to conquer them. (The enemies are self-doubt, low self-confidence, not knowing the difference between guilt and shame, listening to and giving credit to negative self-talk, etc.)

Self-Care

Self-care is taking care of the every-day things in life--but doing so in a purposeful manner. Such things as getting up on time, eating regular meals, and planning something fun are examples.

Two false beliefs that create obstacles to applying self-care are: (1) "I'm too busy to do something for me," and (2) "It's selfish to take time out for me." It is important and helpful to remember that self-care is not the same as selfish care. Selfish care is an OVERemphasis on self. Self-care, on the other hand, brings energy and motivation back into the self so you may have a healthier, balanced relationship with yourself and others and have more to give.

The following chapters describe how to apply all six of these principles of personal balance. Best wishes on your journey to personal health and balance.

3

Trust

All the principles for achieving personal balance intertwine like the strands of a rope. One strand is important, but by itself will not have the strength or endurance to hold you without breaking. A mountain climbing rope is made up of hundreds of slender threads woven into small ropes. The small ropes are interwoven to create a larger rope which can support the weight of several thousand pounds. At the conclusion of this book, you will see how each principle is independently important like a small rope, but how much more strength and endurance your personal "rope" will have as you learn to weave all the principles together to develop a strong, durable personal balance that will support the weight of your life.

There are two foundation principles for developing personal balance. First, when you learn to trust yourself others can more easily trust you. Next you need to learn when and how to trust others.

Without the foundation of trust, you will not have the confidence or belief in yourself to develop and maintain stability in the other principles. If the principles are not in place and stable, you will have difficulty keeping balance and peace with yourself as an individual or in your relationships with others.

Going back to the rope analogy, TRUST is the center strand of your rope; all the other principles for achieving personal balance weave in around it. The more "small ropes" (principles) you weave in to reinforce the center strand, the more secure, durable and beneficial the rope will be in your life.

Burton, a client, is a good example of this concept. When he came in for counseling he was seriously discouraged and frustrated with himself. Several years previously he had heard some friends mention how intrigued they were with porn sites on the Internet. One quiet evening he went to several of the sites his friends had mentioned. He experienced a number of different feelings such as disgust, excitement, physical arousal, and curiosity.

A few days later his curiosity got the best of him and he went again to the same sites and found several others. It wasn't long before he was "hooked," and found himself indulging whenever he had a spare moment alone. Even so, his conscience was strong and after a time he decided to stop. However, he found it hard to discontinue the practice of viewing Internet pornography. After awhile, he became aware that he couldn't **trust** himself to be alone around a computer. He actually began to hate himself and think of himself as weak because he couldn't be trusted alone without looking at pornography. He had become addicted to Internet pornography. At this point he decided to seek out help.

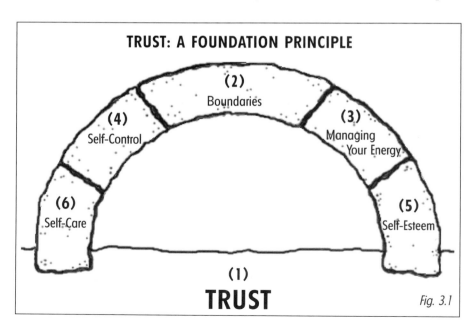

TRUST: A FOUNDATION PRINCIPLE

(2) Boundaries

(4) Self-Control

(3) Managing Your Energy

(6) Self-Care

(5) Self-Esteem

(1) **TRUST**

Fig. 3.1

Burton didn't realize how much time he had been spending on the computer until I had him write down the number of times he viewed pornography and how long he viewed it each time. Because he had been spending the majority of his free time indulging his addiction to pornography, he had become somewhat isolated With a lot of determination and hard work, Burton began to gain back some of his self-confidence as he started regaining control of his life.

Some factors that contribute to developing trust in yourself are:

- Developing a pattern of resolving little problems (an "I can do it" attitude).
- Making decisions and following through with them.
- Taking responsibility for your actions.
- Saying you are sorry when needed and admitting mistakes quickly.
- Being okay with mistakes as long as you learn from them.
- Being aware of your limits.
- Making adjustments to avoid repeating mistakes.
- Gaining an appreciation for yourself (seeing yourself as half-full vs. half-empty).
- Identifying and labeling areas you need to change in your life and making a plan to work on them.
- Staying in the present and not dwelling on the past.
- Saying no when you mean no and sticking to it.

The next worksheet encourages you to make a list of your positive qualities. This can be hard to do, but will be very rewarding. Most people are reluctant to talk about their positive qualities, and may not have considered the positive aspects of their lives. To get started, ask yourself questions such as:

1. What are the things that people say about me that are positive?
2. What things make me feel uplifted after I do them?
3. Who have I helped lately?
4. How did I practice self-control lately?

POSITIVE QUALITIES FOR TRUSTING YOURSELF WORKSHEET

List positive qualities that indicate you are a person to be trusted:

Example: When I make an appointment, I try very hard to be on time.

1. _____

2. _____

3. _____

4. _____

Make a list of things you have been meaning to do or change in your life, but have been putting off for whatever reason(s).

Example: Stop complaining about my wife's cooking behind her back and tell her truthfully about some of the things I don't like.

1. _____

2. _____

3. _____

4. _____

There are three ways to think about trust. First, do I trust myself? Second, am I a person whom others can trust? Third, how do I know when I can trust others? The following questionnaire (twelve traits of a person who can be trusted) will help you answer these questions.

The Twelve Traits of a Person Who Can Be Trusted (the Level of Trust Questionnaire)

The Level of Trust Program is comprised of the twelve traits of a person who can be trusted. A measurement tool is provided at the end of the definitions that will help you answer the three questions posed above. Please keep in mind that this is a questionnaire and not a psychological test; it is a *guide* for relationships.

As you read the definitions that follow, keep in mind that they are meant to be considered as a group. If you are struggling with several of the traits, it does not mean you are an untrustworthy or a bad person. It simply indicates a need for improvement in those particular traits.

1. Security: You will be safe *physically* and *emotionally* when you are with a trustworthy person.

Knowing that someone will always have your best interest in mind and that they would never intentionally harm you physically or emotionally is the basis for feeling secure in relationships. At times, all of us may do something unintentionally that could potentially put stress on a relationship. When this happens, if you have established a strong trusting relationship, and the other person knows you have their best interest at heart, then mistakes can quickly be forgiven and the relationship will continue to grow and become stronger.

Feeling secure in a relationship is like taking the time and care to build a large reserve of money in your bank account that can be considered your "relationship reserve." Having enough money in the relationship reserve with others is the key to building strong, vital, enduring relationships. If you have a large relationship reserve when you make a mistake, it is a small withdrawal, rather than a threat of bankruptcy.

2. Responsibility: Trustworthy people accept responsibility, without excuses, for whatever they say and do.

Responsible people are quick to say they are sorry when they offend someone; they don't make excuses or deny what was said or done, and they do not minimize their actions. A person who is responsible is also conscientious--considerate of others feelings. They discontinue doing anything they learn is offensive to others. When you are a responsible person a lot of pressure is taken off others because they know they won't have to take up the slack for your irresponsibility

3. Honesty: Trustworthy people tell the truth.

When you are trustworthy, others can rely on your words. They do not have to guess what you are saying or read between the lines. Others can relax around you because they will not have to second guess what you say.

4. Dependability: A trustworthy person does not have to be asked two or three times to do what they promised to do.

"Solid, steady and sure" are a few qualities that come to mind when thinking of a person who is dependable. When a dependable person gives their word to do something, you can count on it being done.

Joan of Arc was a prime example of dependability. In the midst of a campaign, she was confronted with an enemy fortress that appeared invincible. Her advisers tried to get her to turn back and break her commitment to lead her people. They exclaimed, "The fortress is too strong and too well protected." But turning back would have let down all who were depending on her.

Joan of Arc made it clear that her choice was to attack and that she herself would be at the front of the charge. Her advisers warned that no one would follow her into battle. She said, "I will not be looking back to find out who is following me." Joan's courage was so inspiring that her army followed her into battle, and they fought so valiantly that they prevailed. She was committed. There was no question in her mind what she needed to do, and as a result of this, others knew they could depend on her.

5. Reverence: Trustworthy people have respect and esteem for people, nature and God.

An advertisement on T.V. showed a man hitchhiking to the nearest gas station because his car had broken down. A person stopped to pick him up and brushed some cans and paper off the seat onto the road to clear a space for him to sit down. The hitchhiker was so upset about the disrespectful act of trash being thrown onto the roadway that he picked the trash up and chose not to accept the ride.

I once read that the decline of a nation is always preceded by the decline of reverence for God, people, and nature-- reverence being defined as a profound respect mingled with love. A quote credited to Carlyle says, "Reverence is the highest of human feelings."

6. Predictability: It is easy to predict what a trustworthy person will say and do because their behavior has been consistently positive over time.

Nobody is perfect. We all make mistakes. Sometimes we all do things we should not. However, a predictably trustworthy person consistently, over time, really tries to do the right thing. They are builders rather than wreckers. When they make a mistake they will more than likely try to correct it. They are not erratic or inconsistent in their behavior. You can count on them to follow through with promises.

7. Values: A trustworthy person has a set of positive standards which govern what they say and do.

Values are those things a person holds most dear. They are not open to much negotiation or change. There are religious values, work values, family values, moral values, and more. They are the fingerprint of who you are and what you stand for.

A person who can be trusted will include in their value system a high regard and esteem for others. A trustworthy person will have high standards for what they say and do. They would never purposefully hurt someone physically, emotionally, or spiritually.

8. Positive body language: A trustworthy person will look you in the eye; they will face you directly when talking to you; their body language is congruent with their attitude.

When your child comes to you with head bowed and eyes looking down at the floor, it is a pretty good indicator something is wrong. Similarly, when someone avoids eye contact while talking with you, you should be cautious. A person who is relaxed around you and looks you in the eye suggests they have nothing to hide.

9. Respectable reputation: A trustworthy person has usually gained the respect of a significant number of people over a long period of time.

On occasion, I will have a person challenge me about this trait because of a bad experience with a spouse who, from all outward appearances, was a pillar of the community, but privately, at home, was described by the spouse as a "monster."

The problem is usually a failure to consider the over-all picture. Although each trait is important in and of itself, a trustworthy person will embrace many of the traits and be consistent in using them—with family as well as others. In other words, the more traits a person exemplifies and the more frequently/consistently a person uses them, the more likely it will be that you can trust that person.

10. Accurate face value: What you see is what you get. There are no hidden agendas.

It is so refreshing to deal with a person you can trust--one with no hidden agendas. What you see is consistently what you get.

My wife once asked me to pick up a specific brand and type of beans at the store. I was very careful to follow directions and read the labels on the cans so I would get exactly what she requested. I dutifully delivered the can of beans with a smile, and patted myself on the back for a job well done. Later in the day, my wife came to me with a look of disbelief on her face. The contents of the can were totally different from what the label said was inside. Ask yourself this question: "Is what I present to others outwardly truly representative of who I am inside?"

11. Positive attitude: A trustworthy person focuses on the positive and consistently expresses, and shows appreciation.

Everyone has bad days or may even have a down period in their lives. However, you always have the choice whether to see life as being half empty or half full. I once heard someone make a statement attributed to John Homer Miller:

"Your living is determined not so much by what life brings to you as by the attitude you bring to life; not so much by what happens to you as by the way your mind looks at what happens. Circumstances and situations do color life, but you have been given the mind to choose what the color shall be."

12. Loyalty: A trustworthy person knows your strengths and weaknesses and builds on your strengths and will support you in overcoming your weaknesses.

Some years ago, I worked with a client who had grown up with Attention Deficit Disorder (ADD). He had struggled mightily to graduate from high school, and finally succeeded. His parents were very much opposed to his going on to college or technical school because they did not believe he should "push his luck." For years his parents had called him dumb and stupid and told him he would never amount to anything.

His siblings were all very bright; several were Sterling Scholars. His parents allowed his siblings to run him down; all but one participated in this humiliating and disgraceful activity. This person, an older sister, demonstrated great loyalty to him; she took him under her wing and became one of his mentors. Similarly, a high school teacher saw the need and became one of his best friends and supporters. In spite of his disability, and in part due to the loyalty of these two individuals, he blossomed and discovered hidden talents no one before had looked long enough to discover. For example, he discovered he could take almost anything apart, fix it, and put it back together again. He had a winning smile and great sense of humor when you got to know him.

You can imagine how this story might have turned out if no one had mentored him, if no one had seen his strengths but had rather focused on the obvious weaknesses instead. A trustworthy person is a builder, not a wrecker. A trustworthy person will not exploit your weaknesses nor broadcast them in front of others. For example, a trustworthy person will discuss a concern about his spouse only when the spouse is present.

Using the Level of Trust Questionnaire *(Individual)*

Purpose:

The Level of Trust Questionnaire (Individual) measures how trustworthy you see yourself when measured by the twelve traits of a person who can be trusted. The author asked hundreds of people what traits they thought a "trustworthy" person would have. The traits used in this questionnaire are based on their answers. **Read the directions carefully before answering the questions.**

Directions:

The Level of Trust Questionnaire-Individual (LTQ-I) uses three levels of trust to determine trust in relationships; Level one: Indicates a person who can be trusted; Level two: Indicates a need for improvement or caution in how you treat others; Level three: Indicates you have serious problems in how you treat others. Follow the steps below:

1. Read the twelve traits of a person who can be trusted.
2. Read the brief definition of the twelve traits.
3. Go to the LTQ-I and answer the questions.
4. Go to the page titled "Directions for Scoring the LTQ-I" (p. 32) and follow the instructions.

LEVEL OF TRUST QUESTIONNAIRE - INDIVIDUAL (LTQ-I)*

Answer the following questions using this scale:

4	3	2	1	0
Never	Rarely	Sometimes	Frequently	Almost Always

Do you:

Scoring Column

1. Keep things out in the open without hidden agendas? _____
2. Behave in ways that others say they can rely on? _____
3. Have a positive reputation with family and friends in the community? _____
4. Have respect for nature, people, and God? _____
5. Refuse to be dishonest, even when tempted? _____
6. Help and support others in overcoming their problems? _____
7. Follow through with promises? _____
8. Take responsibility for what you say and do? _____

Answer each of the following questions using this scale:

4	3	2	1	0
Almost Always	Frequently	Sometimes	Rarely	Never

Do you:

9. Share friend's secrets with others? _____
10. Say one thing and then do something else? _____
11. Make fun of others? _____
12. Use guilt to manipulate others? _____
13. Behave in ways others say are negative? _____
14. Break confidences? _____
15. Make negative and unkind statements to others? _____
16. Expect the worse from yourself or others? _____

SIX PRINCIPLES FOR ACHIEVING PERSONAL BALANCE

Answer each of the following questions using this scale:

8	7	6	5	0
Almost Always	Frequently	Sometimes	Rarely	Never

Do you:

17. Often have others question your behavior and character? _____
18. Force others to be involved with you against their will? _____
19. Try to dominate your friends' time and dictate who they associate with? _____
20. Use intimidation to control what others say or do? _____
21. Tell lies about yourself or others? _____
22. Use language others say is vulgar? _____
23. Monopolize your friend's time and don't want them to do things with others? _____
24. Treat friends or family mean when alone with them, but nice when in the presence of others? _____
25. Withhold affection from loved ones to control them? _____
26. Have a pattern of being secretive about what you do? _____

Answer each of the following questions using this scale:

4	3	2	1	0
Never	Rarely	Sometimes	Frequently	Almost Always

Do you:

27. Focus on positive things? _____
28. Look others in the eyes and face them while talking to them? _____
29. Protect your family and friends physically and emotionally? _____
30. Consistently show support and positive attention to family and friends? _____
31. Have a set of positive values that dictates what you say and do? _____
32. Show an interest in what your family and friends do? _____

Answer each of the following questions using this scale:

4	3	2	1	0
Almost Always	Frequently	Sometimes	Rarely	Never

Do you:

33. Follow through with obligations/commitments inconsistently? _____
34. Get accused of not being honest? _____
35. Make negative or judgmental comments to others? _____
36. Want to be the center of everyone's attention? _____
37. Lie to others about where you have been? _____

Total points from page one and page two _____

* The LTQ-I is not a psychological test for use as a professional tool at this stage in its development. However, it can be used as a valuable *guide* to consider aspects of trusting relationships.

Directions for scoring the LTQ-I

Add up the scoring column for both pages and write it on the "total points" line on page two of the LTQ-I.

LEVEL OF TRUST INDICATORS

The level of trust indicators are provided to suggest the level of trust in your relationships based on your score from the LTQ-I. Following is a suggested range of levels.

0 to 80   Scores in this range indicate that you believe you are a trustworthy person.

81 to 140   Scores in this range indicate a need for improvement in your relationships with others. The closer to 140, the more cautious others will probably be around you.

141 to 188 Scores in this range indicate serious problems and trust issues in your relationships with others. The closer to 188, the more serious this problem is and the more people will beware when they are with you.

Years ago I heard a quote attributed to Ralph Waldo Emerson, it stated, "What lies behind us and what lies before us are tiny matters compared to what lies within us." As you study and learn about the personal balance principles, you will see how they all fit together and especially why trust is such an important asset to build upon. Being able to trust yourself is paramount to being a person who can be trusted in a relationship.

In Chapter Four, you will learn about boundaries in relationships. As you go through the six principles of personal balance again, imagine that you are constructing a sturdy rope. Each strand is important, but the more strands/ principles you weave into your rope, the stronger and more durable it will become.

Notes and Insights

4

Self-boundaries in Relationships

Robert Frost made the profound statement, "Good fences make good neighbors." A fence indicates a boundary, but what is a boundary? A boundary indicates or fixes limits. While all healthy relationships have boundaries, placement of those boundaries differ according to personal needs. One person might be shocked and feel a violation of their personal space if they were hugged. Another person might feel left out and disappointed if they were not hugged. Boundaries define how you distinguish yourself from others physically and emotionally—how you define your own accountability and let others have theirs. Boundaries also protect your right to make your own choices and keep yourself safe.

Another way to conceptualize boundaries is to think of the life of a cell within the body. Every cell has an outer membrane called a cell wall that is the cell's boundary. The cell wall has the important role of *discriminating* what it lets in and what it lets out. For example, if the cell wall doesn't let oxygen in, the cell will die. Once the cell uses the oxygen it has, it must let the by-product (carbon dioxide) out because the used oxygen is now a toxin to the cell. If the toxin isn't let out and disposed of, the cell will die.

Similarly, for relationships to be healthy, you must learn to discriminate what to let in and out. How you set and manage a relationship boundary can bring order and peace to your life, or chaos and wreckage. So, *good boundaries* make *good relationships*.

This chapter will set the basis for relationships with others by focusing on the relationship you have with yourself. If, for whatever reason(s) you are personally out of balance, your important relationships will likely be out of balance as well.

The Relationship Continuum

It is **N**ormal, **N**atural, and **N**ecessary to have acquaintances, friends, and close friends. Without these relationships, you will be isolated and have difficulty achieving balance and happiness in your life. The following diagram (*Fig. 4.1*) introduces the *step function*, which moves people along the Relationship Continuum.

Acquaintances are people you don't know well. You may say "hi" once in a while or even know the person's name. An example might be a person who works in your building that you occasionally ride the elevator with. Although you know each other, you don't get together or "hang out" with one another.

A **friend** is more than an acquaintance. From your pool of acquaintances there will be those you have more in common with and enjoy being with more than others; at some point you ask these special acquaintances to do something with you, for example, to go bowling. Once you start spending time doing things with acquaintances that *steps* them up to the friend level. It is good to have many friends.

A **close friend** is someone you have learned to trust because you can mutually share personal information with one another and that trust is not violated. It is the risk factor of sharing and receiving of personal information that *steps* a friend to the close friend level. Trust and loyalty also exist in close relationships.

All healthy relationships begin with the relationship you have with yourself. The foundation of a healthy relationship with self is based on how you manage

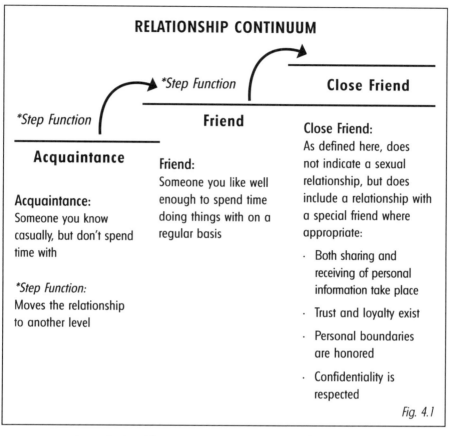

RELATIONSHIP CONTINUUM

*Step Function

Close Friend

*Step Function

Friend

Acquaintance

Acquaintance:
Someone you know
casually, but don't spend
time with

Step Function:
Moves the relationship
to another level

Friend:
Someone you like well
enough to spend time
doing things with on a
regular basis

Close Friend:
As defined here, does
not indicate a sexual
relationship, but does
include a relationship with
a special friend where
appropriate:

· Both sharing and
  receiving of personal
  information take place

· Trust and loyalty exist

· Personal boundaries
  are honored

· Confidentiality is
  respected

Fig. 4.1

your personal needs. In Chapter One I introduced the concept of identifying your personal needs and then developing a plan to meet them in healthy ways. (see *The Needs You Have as an Individual*, p. 10).

A few examples might help clarify this point. If a person has diabetes, some ways of meeting the personal needs to be healthy include:

1. Taking a fasting blood sugar count each morning before eating
2. Keeping the blood sugar count between 80 and 120 as much as possible
3. Keeping the carbohydrate count to around 50 grams per meal
4. Having quarterly check-ups with a medical doctor
5. Staying on prescribed medications
6. Exercising regularly

Balancing Boundaries

What happens if the person with diabetes knows the above principles for the healthy management of the illness but chooses not to do them? Choosing not to follow prescribed behaviors would constitute a self-boundary violation.

Boundary violations have negative consequences on the relationship a person has with himself or herself such as:

- being cross and irritable
- experiencing guilt
- feeling depressed
- developing a lowered self-esteem
- developing poor physical health
- dwelling on negative or self-defeating thoughts
- developing addictive behaviors
- Choosing isolation

On the other hand, when a person chooses to follow the prescribed healthy behaviors for diabetes, the potential for a longer, healthier life is much improved. This would be an example of good healthy self-boundaries.

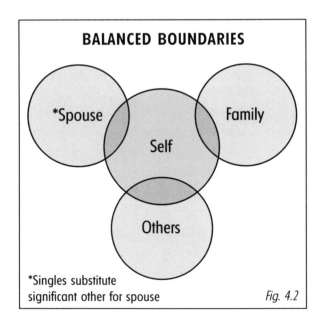

BALANCED BOUNDARIES

*Spouse

Family

Self

Others

*Singles substitute
significant other for spouse

Fig. 4.2

The diagrams (*Fig. 4.2 – 4.4*) depict the basic relationships in life from both balanced and out-of-balance boundary perspectives. All healthy relationships have boundaries. The first diagram illustrates an overall healthy, balanced relationship.

Keep in mind that no one's relationships with self and others are perfectly balanced or have such good boundaries as the diagram above illustrates. The important thing is to realize *when* your boundaries are not in good balance. The next two diagrams (*Fig. 4.3 and Fig. 4.4*) depict what happens when relationships with others get out of balance.

Figure 4.3 depicts an OVERemphasis on relationships with others (all relationships outside of your family) at the expense of the relationship with the spouse and family members (children, parents, grandparents, etc.). OVERemphasizing one relationship often results in OBS.

The last diagram on this page (*Fig. 4.4*) depicts the family pattern of a neighbor family I had when growing up. The children of this family were left alone every weekend and most week nights because the parents were out together away from home. The children had very little supervision and ended up getting into a lot of trouble. Even with the children getting into trouble, the parents did not change their behavior, and the children continued having problems throughout their school years.

It is important to remember that whenever you are *out of balance*,

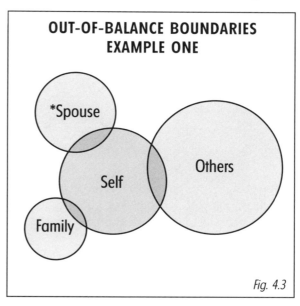

OUT-OF-BALANCE BOUNDARIES EXAMPLE ONE

Fig. 4.3

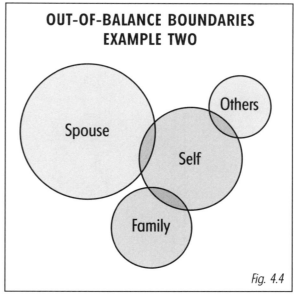

OUT-OF-BALANCE BOUNDARIES EXAMPLE TWO

Fig. 4.4

you will be prone to think, say, and do things that are not healthy for the relationship you have with yourself and others. When boundary violations occur, negative consequences always follow, for example: shame, deterioration in relationships, separation/divorce, depression, and, sometimes, addictive behaviors.

Consider the example of Tess, who was down on herself because she didn't think she could do anything well. She was so worried about doing something wrong, she actually became mistake-ridden. She was so obsessed with her mistakes she didn't recognize the good things she was accomplishing, and she began to distrust herself. In a sense, her focus on her mistakes and putting herself down was a form of self-boundary violation. Focusing so much on the negative in one's life is damaging to your *self*, and will get in the way of how you relate to everyone in your life, including yourself.

On the following pages you will find several worksheets designed to help you assess the boundaries in your life and make changes in areas where you may be out of balance. Tess's situation will be used as the example for this next worksheet.

SELF-BOUNDARIES WORKSHEET

It is necessary to maintain balance in our lives by protecting our boundaries and learning to discriminate between issues, feelings, and behaviors which are our own, and those that belong to others. This worksheet will help you identify a self-boundary violation and write a plan to correct it.

Examples of self-boundary violations could include: putting yourself down, over-eating, dwelling on negative thoughts, consistently staying up too late, etc.

Identify a self-boundary that you have violated. (Start by listing only two.)

Example: Dwelling on and obsessing too much about my mistakes.

1. _____

_____

_____

2. _____

_____

_____

Develop a plan to prevent future self-boundary violations and set a date to implement your plan.

Example: This weekend, I will take a 3x5 card and write on it "STOP" dwelling on my mistakes. I will also put something positive about myself on the card. I will put the card in my pocket. When I am tempted to dwell on a mistake, I will pull the card out to help remind me to think of something positive about myself instead.

_____

_____

_____

_____

Date _____

Tess wondered where her negative attitude came from. As we discussed her background, it became apparent that she grew up in a *very* critical environment. Her mother never complimented her and always had a critical comment to make about Tess's performance. As a result she took on the belief that she couldn't do anything well enough. Following is how she diagrammed her family dynamics. This will give you an idea of how to prepare your own diagram on the following worksheet:

Make a diagram depicting your family dynamics while growing up.

Example:

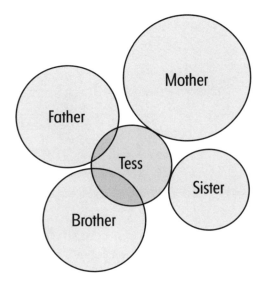

FAMILY BOUNDARIES WORKSHEET

Using diagrams 4.2, 4.3, & 4.4 for ideas, draw diagrams for the two following exercises. There should be a circle representing every member in your family. Notice diagrams 4.2-4.4 use self as the center and show other relationships in reference to your relationship with them.

Make a diagram depicting your family dynamics while growing up.

How did this impact your adolescence?

_____

_____

_____

_____

_____

Make a diagram depicting your present situation. (For example, if you are single, your family would be your family of origin, if you are married, then it would be your present family.)

What changes would you like to make?

_____

_____

_____

_____

_____

RELATIONSHIP BOUNDARIES WORKSHEET

It is necessary to express your feelings and set limits in order to establish and maintain personal balance and have healthy relationships with others.

Everyone has the right to refuse responsibility that rightly belongs to someone else. Appropriate boundaries bring true freedom and true balance to the relationship. Use this worksheet to identify a relationship where you have allowed someone to take advantage of you.

Identify a relationship in which a boundary has been violated.

Example: *My mother is constantly putting me down.*

_____

_____

_____

Identify the boundary that has been violated.

Example: *When my mother calls me fat.*

_____

_____

_____

List the steps that you can take if a boundary violation occurs again.
(Use, "When you...I feel...because...next time...")

Example: *When you call me fat I feel hurt and angry because I am already so self-conscious about my weight. Next time...*

1. _____
2. _____
3. _____
4. _____
5. _____

Develop a plan to prevent future boundary violations in this relationship.

Example: *Plan ahead what I will say and do before visiting with my mother, so when she makes negative remarks I will be ready and not be caught off guard.*

_____

_____

_____

_____

_____

In addition to the worksheets in this chapter, go back to the *Individual Needs Worksheet* (Chapter One, pg. 10) and follow through with a need you have identified. If you have completed the worksheet, identify another need and follow through with it. If you haven't completed the worksheet, do so now and follow through with it.

Here are some suggested exercises to strengthen your boundaries:

1. For twenty-four hours, keep track of how you meet your needs. For example, if you feel exhausted, do you rest immediately or just keep going and pushing harder? (Use the first journal included at the end of this chapter, p. 42, for this exercise.)
2. For the next twenty-four hours, purposefully choose to meet each emotional need without hesitating and do so as fully as possible. For example, if you are lonely, call a friend to hang out with. If you are frustrated, find someone you trust to talk to. If you are stressed, arrange for a massage. If you are happy, celebrate with someone. (Use the second journal included at the end of this chapter, p. 43, for this exercise.)

Be patient with yourself. Cleaning up old boundary problems will take time but the rewards are enormous and well worth the effort. Keep in mind; it may benefit you to seek the help of a professional counselor to help you identify areas you need help in. A counselor can help support you through boundary work, which can be pretty intense. You may also want to do some reading on the subject. A book I recommend is: *Boundaries: Where You End and I Begin* by Anne Katherine ([1993], New York: Simon & Schuster).

In reality, all of the principles for achieving balance focus on the relationship you have with yourself. Personal balance is important, because in order for you to have success in relationships with others, you must *first* achieve personal balance.

Understanding the concepts taught in each chapter, doing the worksheets, and applying what you have learned will be a big step in creating personal balance in your life. Chapter Five will introduce you to energy management, part of which is learning to identify unresolved conflicts in your life, and how to bring more peace into your life.

JOURNAL ONE

date	starting time	ending time

Need	**Type of Need**	**How you met the need**
	physical, spiritual, emotional, social	
Example:		
Stronger self-confidence		*Put a card in my purse with positive*
	Emotional	*statements about myself and to remind*
		myself not to dwell on the negative.

When you felt exhausted, did you rest or did you just keep going and/or push harder

Go to p. 41 for detailed instructions for using this journal.

JOURNAL TWO

date	starting time	ending time

Emotional Need	How you met the need

Go to p. 41 for detailed instructions for using this journal.

Notes and Insights

5

Energy and Conflict Management

When you think of the term *energy*, many things might come to your mind such as: nuclear energy, potential energy, available power, vigorous activities, a powerful force, or something with great potential. Personal energy is a precious commodity that must be understood and protected; otherwise it can be inadequately used or misused. In the following pages you will be introduced to five steps that will help you manage your energy. At the end of the chapter you will find a worksheet for applying what you have learned about managing your energy. You will also learn in this chapter how emotional conflicts take away energy from your daily life. Let's begin by taking a look at the first step.

Step One – A Typical Day

Some days you may get up and feel like you have only 85% of your total energy to give to your day because you didn't sleep well, or you were up worrying about something. Even so, think of yourself as a 100% system. Every morning when

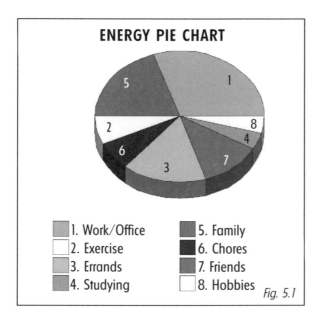

ENERGY PIE CHART

1. Work/Office
2. Exercise
3. Errands
4. Studying
5. Family
6. Chores
7. Friends
8. Hobbies

Fig. 5.1

you get up, in a sense, you carve up that 100% into activities that take your time and energy. Look now at the energy pie chart (*Fig. 5.1*). This is an example of the time and energy spent on a typical day's activities. The next step introduces how unresolved conflict takes away energy.

Step Two – Unresolved Conflict

Conflict is a mental struggle resulting from unresolved needs, drives, wishes, or external or internal demands. Unresolved conflict in your life takes energy away from your 100% system and leaves you with less to give to your day. This chapter focuses on the skill of identifying which conflicts in your life you can control, and what to do to resolve them. For example, if your parent is not talking to you and you are feeling upset, you have control over your own feelings of anger, but you have no control over the parent. So it is your anger that you need to resolve.

When you are not able to resolve an angry feeling it becomes stored negative energy. In the next chapter we will discuss how unresolved feelings escalate if you do not deal with them soon after the triggering incident. If left unresolved, the conflict(s) takes energy away from you, leaving you with less capacity to deal with your daily responsibilities, especially in the important relationships in your life.

Janice's situation illustrates the point. She complained of being tired, lethargic, and exhausted. At night she would toss and turn, worrying, not being able to turn her mind off. This only added to her mental and physical fatigue. Janice talked about all the "loose ends" in her life that she had never been able to tie up. When I presented her with the energy concept she estimated that she was using 35-40 percent of her energy on unresolved conflicts in her life. As a result, she never felt at peace. She was cross and irritable towards her children and husband; she didn't want to act this way, but couldn't seem to help herself. Janice admitted she had begun feeling quite discouraged and sensed she was becoming depressed.

I had Janice identify (and write down) the conflicts she was struggling with; it turned out to be a long list. It was no wonder she was feeling so exhausted and discouraged. As we looked over the list, it was apparent that some of the conflicts she struggled with were not within her control, such as her husband not wanting to go to church with her, or her daughter wanting to spend time with friends rather than with her. On the other hand, there were a number of conflicts she could have more control over if she were to be more mindful, such as: getting up on time to go to work, being calm or acting angry when disciplining the children, exercising, diet, etc.

As we considered the conflicts she could have more control over, she came up with the idea to get up earlier so she could have breakfast with her daughter. As she assessed her schedule she also realized that she never took time for herself and that she had let several fun hobbies go over the years. When she thought about taking time for a hobby or two she became excited; when she actually made time to do her hobbies she felt less depressed, more energetic, and more balanced.

If there are unresolved conflicts in your life, you may be using 25% or more of your energy to cope with those conflicts--taking away from energy you have left to give to your planned activities. Say for example, you are using 25% of your "Pie" to cope with unresolved conflicts. This leaves you with only 75% to use for your day. Take some time to think of any unresolved conflicts you might have in your life at this time. *Figure 5.2* (next page) lists examples of typical conflicts that, when unresolved, take energy away from you.

Step Three – Estimated Conflict Percentage (%)

Now that you have thought about some of the unresolved conflicts in your life, take a moment to estimate what percentage of your energy is being spent on these unresolved conflicts. Most people are surprised, at how much estimated energy is going towards conflicts that are not resolved. Taking these steps helps in many ways:

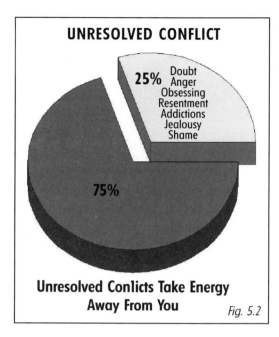

UNRESOLVED CONFLICT

25% Doubt
Anger
Obsessing
Resentment
Addictions
Jealousy
Shame

75%

**Unresolved Conlicts Take Energy
Away From You**

Fig. 5.2

1. Instead of stumbling in the dark wondering why you are feeling frustrated, fatigued, and overwhelmed, you will identify and label your unresolved conflicts.
2. Writing the conflict down heightens your awareness of it.
3. Estimating the percentage of energy expended on it will help you get in touch with the impact of the unresolved conflicts on your daily life.

The estimated percentage gives you a goal to keep in mind so you can work towards bringing more energy back to your daily activities. Don't spend too much time at this point trying to figure out an exact percentage. You will have the opportunity later in the chapter to put more thought into it. The next step looks at resolution ideas.

Step Four – Resolution/Personal Balance

Step four focuses on strategies to resolve your conflict(s). Learning the Six Principles for Achieving Personal Balance and how to use them will help you develop powerful and useful strategies to resolve the conflicts in your life. All of the principles below have either been introduced in previous chapters or will be introduced in the following chapters. These strategies compliment one another, and as you apply them, these principles work together like the strands of a rope.

1. Trust
2. Boundaries
3. Managing your energy
4. Self-control (using the Thought Shield, and mindfulness)

5. Self-worth and self-esteem
6. Self-care

Step Five – Benefits of Resolving Conflicts

There are many benefits that come with the resolution of conflict in your life. When you resolve and let go of conflict you are rejuvenated and energy returns and can be used *differently*. Some benefits that result from the resolution of conflict include:

- Enhanced creativity
- Better problem solving
- Improved rational thinking
- Improved coping skills
- Less fatigue
- Improved relationships

The key word for this step is "differently." Resolving a conflict and behaving differently, brings new, positive energy back to you. The challenge then is to use that energy differently, rather than giving it back to another conflict. When you begin using the Six Principles for Achieving Personal Balance in resolving conflicts, you will begin experiencing the benefits mentioned. This is energy that you can use differently, especially when you apply mindfulness (see Chapter Six). You can watch the percentage increase in the resolved box and decrease in the conflict box.

Jeffrey is an example of how a destructive unresolved conflict can carry over in adult life. Because Jeffrey's father spent little time with him when he was young, he was filled with resentment towards his father. He saw other fathers spending time with their sons and teaching them how to throw and catch the football, taking them hiking and going on overnight camping trips. Even though he often begged his father to do things with him, his father always had excuses. He longed to do things with his father but it happened so infrequently that when they finally did something together he didn't enjoy it because he was so angry and resentful.

Now, as an adult, he had a chip on his shoulder and was constantly unhappy. He was spending an enormous amount of time dwelling on the past and having resentful feelings towards his father. When he started to fill out his energy system worksheet he was amazed at how much of his energy he was giving away to his unresolved resentful feelings towards his father. He estimated he was loosing 40 to 50 percent of his energy to his resentment, depending on the day. It was no wonder he was feeling tired and exhausted all the time.

After Jeffrey set up goals on his worksheet to think and act differently he began to resolve this enormous conflict in his life and to bring the energy back to be used in more productive ways in his life.

Next, you will learn how to set up a worksheet to look at a typical day.

ENERGY SYSTEM WORKSHEET

This worksheet has been designed to take you through each of the five steps that will help you better manage how and where your energy is going. Take your time working through this worksheet.

Step One – A Typical Day

List the activities you participate in on a typical day. Once you have done this assign each one the percentage of your whole energy pie that you think you use up in that activity. Graph those percentages on the pie chart.

Activity   **%**

☐ 1 _____   ____

☐ 2 _____   ____

☐ 3 _____   ____

☐ 4 _____   ____

☐ 5 _____   ____

☐ 6 _____   ____

☐ 7 _____   ____

☐ 8 _____   ____

Step Two – Unresolved Conflict

Make a detailed, but short list of conflicts that are presently not resolved in your life: ***Example:** Feeling resentful towards my father.*

1. _____

2. _____

3. _____

4. _____

Step Three – Estimated Conflict Percentage (%)

Estimate the percentage of your energy going to the unresolved conflict(s) that you listed and write it in the box provided below.

Estimated Conflict %

Step Four – Resolution/Personal Balance

Discuss how you can apply the principles discussed in the previous chapters to help you in resolving conflict in your life.

Example: *Just because my father didn't spend time with me doesn't mean I can't do differently with my own children. My father didn't have good boundaries; he let his work take over his life and consequently I got left out. I will create boundaries between my home life and work, by leaving my work at the office and giving my wife and children my undivided attention while I am at home.*

Step Five – Benefits of Resolving Conflicts

The "Estimated Resolution" box is used in conjunction with the "Estimated Conflict" box. The sum of both boxes must equal 100%. For example, if you wrote 60% in the estimated conflict box, you would write 40% in the estimated resolution box. Write your estimated percentages in the boxes and keep track of how you are doing. An example of healthy balance between unresolved and resolved conflict might be 15/85 respectively.

Estimated Conflict %

TRACKING SHEET

Date	Estimated Conlict (%)	Estimated Resolution (%)	Notes

Conflict Management

Unresolved conflicts in life are inevitable. One key in being able to resolve conflict is learning not to personalize the conflict. For example, if your spouse forgets to pick you up after an appointment and you personalize this incident, you might think, "He didn't pick me up on time; that must mean he doesn't care about me anymore." or "He purposefully forgot to pick me up because he's angry with me about something." In reality, it could be a case of honest forgetfulness, and if it is a case of forgetfulness, it certainly requires an apology, but it doesn't necessarily mean that the relationship is in danger. It is best to check the meaning of an incident rather than make assumptions.

Another problem that can seriously complicate resolving a conflict is catastrophising it (i.e. believing that what has happened or what you think might happen will be so awful that you won't be able to bear it). Catastrophising is a form of seeing things half empty or anticipating the worst possible scenario.

It is more productive to:

1. Ask yourself after an incident what you have learned that can help you in the future.

and

2. Plan ahead for potential conflicts, identifying those things you can control vs. those things you cannot, consequently putting your planning and energy toward those things that are controllable.

Finally, leaving conflicts unresolved is an energy drain which leads inevitably to discouragement, low self-esteem (see Chapter Seven), anger, resentment, and more. Learning to identify unresolved conflicts is a skill that can be learned with practice. This skill is enhanced by the use of mindfulness (see Chapter Six). Facing conflicts often takes courage but is the best course to take once you have identified which conflicts you have some control over. Chapter Six looks at ways to gain self-control by using a very effective tool, the Thought Shield. Using this tool creates another strand in your strong rope of personal balance.

Carefully and honestly analyze each conflict you identified in Step Two of the *Energy Systems* Worksheet. As you think and study the conflicts you identified earlier in the chapter, you will find that you have very little control over some of the identified conflicts. First, identify the source of each conflict (Step One below). Is it about a problem in a relationship, dissatisfaction with a low paying job, health problems, or difficulty letting go of obsessive thoughts or behavior? Next, use the following exercise to help determine the amount of control you have over your conflict(s) (Step Two).

CONFLICT MANAGEMENT WORKSHEET

Step One:

1. Identify and describe each of the conflicts you identified earlier on the *Energy Systems Worksheet* in Step 2:

_____

_____

_____

_____

_____

_____

_____

Step Two:

Determine what parts of each conflict you have control over.

A. Things I cannot control	B. Things I can control
Examples: When others say mean things to me.	How I react to what is said.

<u>Note</u> – Do both Step One and Step Two for each conflict from the *Energy Systems Worksheet.*

Step Three:

Make a commitment to yourself to focus your energy on resolving these conflicts, using only the ones you have control over.

Conflict Plan: Make a plan detailing how you will resolve each conflict and when. *EXAMPLE: How I will react differently to what is said to me:*

1. I will take note of what others say to me, but realize each occurrence is just that person's opinion.
2. If I have made a mistake, I will own up to it and apologize, but I will not dwell on it.
3. I will realize that true friends who have my best interest at heart will give me feedback that doesn't attack my character.

Conflict One Plan: _____
         1. _____
         2. _____
         3. _____
         4. _____

Conflict Two Plan: _____
         1. _____
         2. _____
         3. _____
         4. _____

Conflict Three Plan: _____
         1. _____
         2. _____
         3. _____
         4. _____

Congratulations on completing principle three. You are much closer to learning how to achieve personal balance. The next chapter teaches the principle of self-control.

Notes and Insights

6

Self-control

One of the best ways to boost self-worth and build trust in yourself is to take control of your life--never an easy thing to do. Taking back control can be especially daunting if you have created a dependency with a long-standing habit.

Are you struggling with a persistent habit that just won't go away? One reason old habits die hard is that you become dependent on them. Let's suppose you lived close to a swamp. If you were to personally start feeding a baby alligator, over time the alligator would see you as its main source of food and would become dependent on you. As the dependency grows and the alligator gets bigger and bigger, it won't go away. In addition to taking the food you offer, it may begin nipping at your hand or tearing at your pocket. Eventually, it may chase you, wanting to swallow you up. At this advanced stage of dependency, you realize that you have "created a monster." Just as the alligator became dependent on you, so you have become dependent on your bad habit. The bad habit, just like the alligator, will not go away easily.

A dependency couldn't develop if we refused to feed the alligator to begin with. However, we all tend to over-estimate our ability to stop a behavior, just as we over-estimate both our physical and emotional strength and endurance.

Take a minute and try an experiment. Before starting, guess how long you think you can hold a heavy book on your hand without bending your arm and/or dropping the book. Write the estimated time on a piece of paper. Now, get a heavy book and place it in your hand. Next, extend your arm straight out from your shoulder with your fingers extended and your palm up with the book resting on your palm. See how long you can actually hold the book before you are too tired and have to put it down. Time yourself. What did you discover? Was the task harder than you expected? Most people are amazed how hard this is to do and usually over-guess how long they can hold the book up. Similarly, how often do you over-estimate how strong you will be when faced with a temptation? (Temptation can be anything from saying no to a second donut, to sleeping in and missing a class at school because you are tired, to venting your anger at your boss even though you know there is a chance it will cost you your job.)

Another experiment will illustrate a similar point. Set a timer for ninety seconds and hold the book on your hand, with your arm extended, for that period of time. When the timer rings, rest for ten seconds, then hold the book on your hand for another ninety seconds. Repeat this exercise three or four times. You will notice that the experiment gets increasingly harder to perform with each try. Many people have the mistaken idea that they can "flirt" with temptation anytime they want and not give in. However, repeated encounters with temptation will weaken your ability to say the magic word, "NO." It becomes increasingly difficult to stop feeding the alligator.

The same principle holds true in regard to controlling emotions. Because of the direct relationship between what you *think* and what you *do*, setting limits on your thoughts early on is the only sure way to stay in control of your actions.

In this chapter we will discuss five tools you can use to develop more self-control.

(1) Thought Shield: a visual image to stop unwanted thoughts.
(2) Mindfulness: consistently and purposefully choosing to think differently and then choosing to behave differently.
(3) Reframing: Identifying negative self-talk and changing it to something more positive and hopeful, using rules discussed later in the chapter.
(4) Stopping/starting: stopping a negative behavior and counterbalancing by starting something positive.

(5) Becoming an impartial and benevolent observer: providing yourself with a nurturing and a caring attitude as you stand back and view life in an impartial way.

These five tools will help you deal with emotional triggers.

Emotional Triggers

Out-of-control emotions make us vulnerable to out-of-control behaviors. Learning to identify triggers of unwanted thoughts is an important step towards controlling unwanted behaviors. An acronym that may help you is STAHL. Here are a few examples:

Stress (needing to relax, feeling anxious, being on edge, feeling overwhelmed)

Tired (sleepy, not feeling rested, or not taking good care of health)

Angry, (angry at self or others)

Hungry (this might include hunger for food, companionship, or friendship)

Lonely, (feeling isolated, wanting affection, or feeling unloved)

If you are feeling vulnerable or having difficulty controlling unwanted thoughts, take a minute and ask yourself if one of the STAHL factors is affecting you. If you already acted upon an unwanted thought, take some time to identify what led you to the behavior. If not, figure out which aspects of STAHL might be affecting you, and take appropriate action. For example, if you are hungry for companionship, find a trusted friend to do something with. If you are stressed and tired, practice some deep relaxation and meditation, then take a nap. Some aspects of STAHL may not apply to you. Think about other emotional triggers you might have and create your own acronym. The key to self-control is stopping the thought quickly so you can mindfully choose to do something different.

The Thought Shield

A common complaint I hear from those who seek counseling is their inability to control or manage their thoughts or emotional triggers. For example, they may be having difficulty controlling angry, tempting, stressful, or self-

THOUGHT SHIELD

M I N D F U L N E S S

STOP

3 S's
1. say STOP
2. spell STOP
3. see STOP

*What your mind dwells on,
your body will act upon.*

MINDFULLNESS

Fig. 6.1
© 2006 James B. Lewis

defeating thoughts. The Thought Shield provides imagery to help you gain more self-control.

A stop sign is a powerful image in many ways. For example, the potential negative consequences for disobeying a stop sign are enormous: you and others could be hurt, someone crippled or killed, expensive damage could be done to automobiles, a ticket could be issued, insurance rates could go up, and more.

A stop sign is usually stuck in the ground or fixed to a pole. A shield, on the other hand, can be used whenever or wherever you are. Close your eyes and picture a stop sign in the form of a shield; doing so makes it more real and strengthens its functions and benefit as well. Being able to imagine a stop sign as a shield may take some practice, so be patient as you learn how to make the image work to stop unwanted thoughts. One of the great benefits of the Thought Shield is that it is not only effective for controlling every-day unwanted thoughts, but also for overcoming bad habits.

Visualize the Detail

For years I have been using a stop sign successfully as the major image for this technique. How many points are there in a stop sign? (Eight.) What color is a stop sign as it faces you? (Red.) What color are the letters of the word "stop?" (White.) Keep these details in mind. The more accurate your image of a stop sign, the easier it is to remember. Following are the instructions for using this powerful tool for controlling unwanted thoughts:

Notice that the Thought Shield image has been enhanced with the sword to better symbolize protection. At the bottom of the diagram, you will see the principle, "what your mind dwells on, your body will act upon." You apply the shield simply by using the three S's:

1. In your mind, you say the word STOP.
2. Then in your mind, you spell the word S T O P (say each letter separately).
3. Finally, again in your mind, practice imaging a full-sized stop sign in the form of a shield with a sword next to it. This image should be large enough to protect your whole body.

Apply Stop, Stop, Stop

By applying the three S's, you temporarily stop the unwanted thought. You keep the thought outside your shield by mindfully choosing to put something else in your mind. It is imperative that you do this step immediately after applying the three S's. If you don't do this step quickly, you run the risk of having the unwanted thought enter your mind again and losing the control you just gained. The new, purposeful thought could be a favorite song, poem, or something calming and healing for you to think about.

Remember, you must use all three S's in order to totally activate the beneficial effects of your Thought Shield. Using the three S's puts you back in control of your thoughts, but only momentarily. You stay in control by *actively* putting other thoughts into your mind that are calming and soothing. It is also important to do something different; for example, if you are sitting down, stand up. If you are watching T.V., get up and go into another room.

Keep in mind the *extremely* important principle: "What your mind dwells on, your body will act upon." One illustration of this principle would be saying something like, "Tonight I am going out to eat steak and shrimp (or think of your favorite food). I can hardly wait! Every time I think about it my mouth starts to water." You may have had similar experiences while thinking about and anticipating a favorite food or dessert. Even though you weren't actually eating the favorite food or dessert, just the anticipation of eating it caused the physiological effect of your mouth watering. Thus, "What your mind dwells on, your body will act upon."

Avoid Dwelling on Unwanted Thoughts

Angry, anxious, doubtful, obsessive, and tempting thoughts can take on a power and energy of their own. If you don't control these thoughts right away, they can become overwhelming. Interestingly, what gives such thoughts power over you is your choice to dwell on them. What feeds and energizes an anxious thought is the act of focusing on the anxious thought. There is an opposite relationship between your self-control and the power of an anxious thought. As you dwell on an anxious thought, its power and energy will go up while your self-control goes down. The longer you keep the thought out of your mind by choosing to think about something different, the less power it will have over you.

This dynamic can be compared to a bullet. As the bullet comes out of the barrel, it has enormous energy (recall an anxious thought and how powerful it was initially). However, as the bullet travels through time and space, its power and energy gradually diminishes until it drops to the earth, powerless. Similarly, the longer you can keep the anxious thought out of your mind and the farther you choose to push it away, the more its power will decrease and your self-control will increase.

Mindfulness (combining imagery with powerful concepts)

Mindfulness is a tool that can be used for keeping negative and destructive thoughts out of your mind. As defined here, mindfulness is *consistently* and *purposefully choosing to think differently and then behave differently. Mindfulness* is a powerful tool for changing unwanted thoughts and behaviors. When combined with the Thought Shield image, mindfulness is even more powerful as a change agent. The act of *consistently* and *purposefully choosing* to stop a thought and putting a different thought in its place, and then purposely doing something different is not only a change agent for your behavior, but, over time, changes how your brain chemistry works.

Being mindful implies not reacting the same negative way to a situation or incident the next time that situation or incident presents itself. In functional terms, it means the ability to learn and analyze. Mindfulness is the ability to go around obstacles, to be creative, to think in new terms about past behavior. When the outcome is positive you can benefit from the experience by practicing mindfulness even better the next time. Mindfulness encompasses imagination or the leap of imagination by which you conquer new and old problems. Mindfulness brings with it the power to prevail. One who is mindful has a strong belief in flexibility and adaptability and the strong desire and belief that change and improvement is possible. If one is mindful, he or she will learn from the past and not get stuck in it. The difference between the past and the future is that the future can be changed, while one can only learn from the past.

Let's go back to the alligator analogy. Consistently using the Thought Shield (i.e. stop feeding it) will stop the alligator in its tracks. With mindfulness, over time, the alligator will start looking elsewhere for food. Even though you stop feeding the alligator, it will periodically come back to test your commitment. Don't feed it again by focusing on the negative thought, because if you do, you will likely start right back where you left off.

Take for example John, who had been struggling for years to control his anger. Even though we were able to discover things from his past that embittered him, he seemed unable to let go of his anger, which had become destructive to his relationships with others. For instance, when a work colleague would suggest how to do something more effectively, John would respond with a defensive remark, return to his office, and slam things around. These outbursts resulted not only in poor work relations, but also his being marked down on his quarterly review, which put his job in jeopardy. In addition, because of his angry outbursts his friends were beginning to shun him; he was becoming a lonely young man. We discovered that his old angry thoughts were enormous triggers that set off a pattern of outbursts that he had difficulty controlling.

I introduced him to the Thought Shield technique. If he could learn to better control his thoughts, he could then apply mindfulness to control the anger that had become so destructive to his relationships. After a few weeks, John was beginning to control the thoughts which triggered his anger. As he gained control over his thoughts, he was able to see that his anger was based on negative incidents from his past that he was taking out on everyone in the present. Being able to stop long enough to think before acting angrily became a real blessing in his life; especially in renewing his relationships with others and forging new relationships.

Two small versions of the Thought Shield are provided at the end of this chapter (pg. 77). Place them in strategic locations to help remind you to use the Thought Shield. On the following page you will find the *Mindfulness Worksheet*. The example on the worksheet relates to Susan, who worried constantly what others thought of her. She was so concerned about the perceptions of others that she would often go to activities that made her uncomfortable rather than decline the invitation. Afterwards, her self-esteem would suffer because she hadn't had the courage to say no. She would feel terrible about herself, replaying in her mind all the reasons she should have said no, and beating herself up for not doing so. By using mindfulness, Susan strongly committed to herself to take a minute to consider the consequences and say no when she didn't want to participate.

This worksheet will help you begin applying the techniques presented in the mindfulness concept. Take your time deciding on a problem you want to change in your life. By doing so, you will be more committed to making the necessary changes.

MINDFULNESS WORKSHEET

Identify a recent thought or behavior to which you *could* have applied mindfulness.

> **Example:** *Saying yes to an invitation to a party when I really wanted to say no.*

Using mindfulness, describe how you could have remained in control and put the unwanted thought or behavior outside of your thought shield.

> **Example:** *When asked if I wanted to attend a party I really didn't want to go to, I could have taken a moment to think over the consequences and then said no.*

Make a plan for applying mindfulness in the future.

> **Example:** *I will commit to mindfully think through my actions and the consequences of saying yes to invitations when I want to say no. I will also use the Thought Shield as I go over the consequences in my mind, remembering this commitment.*

Reframing: A Tool for Changing Negative Self-Talk

To explain this next tool I would like to tell you a story of a young man I will call Steve that I worked with many years ago. One of his buddies told me Steve was quite an artist and I asked him to show me some of his work. He was very talented for a young man of seventeen, and I asked if he would sketch me a picture. A few weeks later Steve brought me an amazing framed black ink picture of a young boy kneeling down on a blanket with a puppy looking up at him. I put it on the wall in my office. I cherish this picture. However, every time I looked at it, I thought *as beautiful as this picture is, there is something wrong with it,* but I couldn't figure out what was wrong. One day my wife came into my office and said, "That's a beautiful picture, but the frame is all wrong for it." Steve had put the black and white picture in an orange frame. I thought, "How could I have missed such as obvious thing?" We took the picture to a professional to have it "reframed"—this time in black which set off the picture nicely. The picture now has a much more positive impact on those who view it.

How you "frame" something (such as a thought) can make an enormous difference on whether it has a positive or negative impact. An example will illustrate the importance of *reframing* negative thoughts.

Example

Frame One:

"I'm probably never going to be able to overcome this problem. Here I am again. Boy, how stupid of me!"

Frame Two (reframing):

"This problem is going to be harder to overcome than I thought. It will be hard, but I know if I keep trying I'll find a way."

Rules for using reframing:

1. Your reframe must be realistic: For example you might say something like, "I know this problem will be difficult to overcome and might take some time but I'm not going to give up."

2. Your reframe must be honest: For example you might say something like, "This is one of the hardest problems I have ever had to deal with; even though I don't have an answer today I will find some solutions."

The purpose of reframing is to change negative thoughts about yourself into more realistic, hopeful, positive ones. Your self-talk has a very powerful influence on you – for positive or negative. Use the worksheet on the following page to practice reframing your thoughts.

REFRAMING WORKSHEET

1. Identify some examples of your negative self-talk.

   Example: *Thinking that I can't do things very well.*

   _____

   _____

   _____

2. Reframe your self-talk to be positive/hopeful.

Negative Self-Talk	**Reframed Self-Talk**
Example: *I don't do things very well.*	**Example:** *I can practice doing things differently.*

   a. _____   a. _____

   b. _____   b. _____

   c. _____   c. _____

   d. _____   d. _____

3. How does your negative self-talk affect your behavior?

   Example: *It decreases my feelings of self-control and pushes my self-esteem down.*

   _____

   _____

   _____

4. How does reframing your self-talk affect your behavior and how you feel about yourself?

   Example: *As I try to do things differently, I find that I am more creative.*

   _____

   _____

   _____

5. How do you feel about yourself after reframing your self-talk?

   Example: *I feel that I am capable of doing much more than I ever thought possible.*

   _____

   _____

   _____

Controlling your self-talk and using positive, affirming thoughts will be a big boost to pushing your self-esteem up and keeping it up.

Stopping/Starting: A tool for stopping unwanted behaviors and starting positive ones

Another helpful tool for dealing with unwanted thoughts/behaviors is called *"stopping – starting."* Some people start doing something positive, but forget to stop doing an associated negative behavior. Others might stop doing something negative, but then forget to start doing something positive.

Any time you stop doing anything negative, it is critical that you counterbalance the *stopping by starting* something positive. Whenever you take a negative behavior out of your negative "bucket" you must put something in your positive "bucket." The void created by taking a behavior out of your negative bucket, if not counterbalanced, will draw you back to fill the void with either the same negative behavior or a new negative behavior.

Think of a negative behavior you have been wanting to stop. Write it down. Now, think of several positive behaviors you can do instead and write them down so when you think of doing the negative behavior you will have other things in mind to do instead.

Negative behavior: _____

List of positive behaviors:

1. _____
2. _____
3. _____

Thought Shield Review

Let's review the process for starting your Thought Shield:

1. Activate your Thought Shield by using the three S's. The three S's stop the unwanted thought and puts it outside your shield.
2. Now, apply mindfulness by actively and purposefully choosing to put another thought in your mind.

3. Then do something physically different (it can be as simple as turning your head or stretching).

It is important to know why the Thought Shield is so effective as compared to other stop-thought techniques. Most recent studies agree that trying to stop a thought by simply putting another thought in your mind is not only ineffective, but can also be counter productive. Two examples make this point:

1. If I were to tell you that for the next minute you cannot think about a pink elephant, (picture a pink elephant in your mind), and asked you at the end of the minute if you were successful, you would probably say that you were unable to think about anything *but* pink elephants.
2. If you had an infected sore on your hand, would you just put a Band-aid on it? Hopefully not. First, you would wash the sore and clean it out. Next, you would put medication on it, followed by a Band-aid to protect it. Finally, you would avoid or prevent the kind of situation that caused the sore in the first place.

Comparing the infected sore to an unwanted thought, and using the Thought Shield, you would stop the infection (unwanted thought) by using the three S's (cleaning the sore). Then you would quickly put another calming, pleasant thought into your mind (medicine) to protect you from the unwanted thought (Band-aid), and then apply mindfulness by choosing to do something different (avoid or prevent situations in which you are most likely to get another sore).

The act of stopping the thought first with the three S's, taking the thought out and symbolically placing it outside your shield, and then keeping it there by using calm, pleasant thoughts is what makes this technique so powerful and effective. Old habits usually take time to extinguish, so don't be discouraged if an unwanted thought seems persistent and doesn't go away immediately. The next worksheet will help you track behaviors you want to stop then apply the Thought Shield to stop that behavior.

THOUGHT SHIELD WORKSHEET

During a 24 hour period, track (1) the frequency (how many times a thought or behavior happens), (2) the duration (once you've had the thought or done the behavior, how long it lasted), and (3) the intensity of the thought or behavior (for example: if you are measuring anger, on a scale of 1 to 10, 1 would be no anger and 10 would be extremely angry). Then list how you decreased frequency, duration, and intensity, by applying the Thought Shield concepts (action).

Thought/Behavior	Frequency	Duration	Intensity
When I forget to do something I have a hard time forgiving myself	Two times a week	1 or 2 hours	1 2 3 4 5 6 7 8 9 10

Action: In the future I will be more mindful of identifying negative self-talk, remind myself that the negative self-talk was just a mistake, and chose to do something positive like taking a walk or reading a book.

1 2 3 4 5 6 7 8 9 10

Action: _____

_____

_____

_____

1 2 3 4 5 6 7 8 9 10

Action: _____

_____

_____

_____

SIX PRINCIPLES FOR ACHIEVING PERSONAL BALANCE

1 2 3 4 5 6 7 8 9 10

Action: _____

_____

_____

1 2 3 4 5 6 7 8 9 10

Action: _____

_____

_____

Escalation Theory

What happens when you dwell on unwanted thoughts?

Intense feelings, if focused upon over a period of time, will usually translate into some kind of physiological action by your body. Let me explain what I mean by introducing you to a concept I call the Escalation Scale (*Fig. 6.2*).

Have you ever had a little sliver in your finger that you could not extract? It can really irritate you. The sliver is always there and may snag on everything. Eventually, if you do not get the sliver out, it can become infected. If an infection is not treated and taken care of, you could eventually lose the finger; all for the sake of a little sliver.

Feelings are similar in many respects. If you do not take care of a feeling by "getting it out" and talking about it, a feeling of irritation can escalate to frustration. Frustration, if not resolved, can escalate to anger. Anger, if left unresolved, has the potential of escalating to rage. As feelings escalate, a number of things begin happening, such as a decreasing ability to control your behavior. When a person reaches the rage stage, they are often completely out of control.

People who come in for therapy initially report being frustrated and discouraged; they doubt that anyone or anything can help them to control their unwanted thoughts and behaviors because they think they have tried everything and nothing has worked. There is much to be said for having the right information and tools for the job. Techniques such as the Thought Shield and concepts such as Mindfulness can be great tools for regaining control over unwanted thoughts and behaviors. In the next few pages, we will look at how your thoughts and feelings can escalate from minor annoyances to the point where you feel out of control. We will also explore more ways for controlling thoughts in order to avoid this escalation.

Over the years as a therapist, I have spent a great deal of time studying different theories of why people behave the way they behave and how relationships work. I have come to accept the Cognitive Therapy model which espouses the belief that your behaviors are preceded by your thoughts. Simply put, the better control you have over a thought and the interpretation of your thought, the greater potential you will have for controlling your feelings, and consequently, your behavior.

Escalation Scale

Let's take a closer look at the Escalation Scale to develop this concept even more. *Fig. 6.2* illustrates two different ways of understanding how thoughts and feelings escalate. You can see how an individual's interpretation of an event or a thought is modified and *can* escalate to a loss of control. Dwelling on a thought will inevitably lead to a feeling. But you can choose to stop that thought and think of something different before the escalation process gets going. Remember, *"What your mind dwells on, your body will act upon"* (see *Fig. 6.1*).

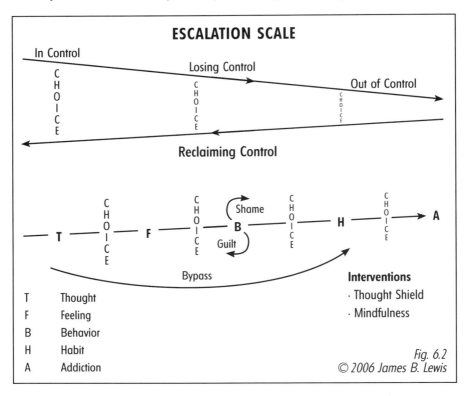

Fig. 6.2
© 2006 James B. Lewis

By way of review, when is the best time to take care of feelings that have the potential to escalate and become intense? As early as possible! This is where the Thought Shield technique comes into play. Go back for a moment and review the Thought Shield technique (p. 57). The key is to identify an *unwanted* thought and stop it early. Otherwise the thought will create a feeling. If you chose to dwell on the feeling, it escalates to a behavior, and continued long enough the behavior can escalate into a habit or even an addiction. An unwanted thought allowed to escalate to an unwanted behavior often causes discouragement and self-doubt. That is why it is so important to apply the Thought Shield early and often to prevent new problems and begin taking back control in areas where problems already exist.

On both diagrams the word "choice" in large letters on the left side decreases in size as feelings escalate. The decrease in choice represents how much more challenging it becomes to apply Mindfulness as we allow ourselves to dwell on unwanted thoughts, as well as how much more limited our choices become. In a sense, as negative feelings escalate, your ability and/or power to choose to stop an unwanted behavior decreases.

Bypass

You will also notice an arrow on the second diagram labeled "bypass." This indicates the choice to disregard mindfulness and skip from a thought to a behavior, habit or addiction, ignoring the consequences that follow. When you catch yourself saying something like, "I don't even remember thinking about it. I just did it," you are bypassing. The goal for defeating a bypass is to apply the Thought Shield, and then use mindfulness quickly and for an extended period. I believe there are several enemies that can get in the way of applying mindfulness and the Thought Shield. Some of these enemies are: doubt, discouragement, and dwelling on the past. If you can remember that the goal is to expand the window of mindfulness (thinking longer before acting on your thoughts) you will be more successful in defeating such enemies. Be patient; bypassing itself might have become a habit, but you *can* defeat it by consistently applying mindfulness and the Thought Shield.

The Difference Between Guilt and Shame

Two by-products result from our negative thoughts or behavior: guilt and shame (see lower diagram of Fig. 6.2)

Guilt

Guilt for a wrong or negative choice is more productive than shame because it usually doesn't lead you to question your character, but instead can lead to meaningful change. While you recognize the fact that you have slipped in your resolve to overcome an unwanted behavior, you don't get stuck dwelling on the mistake; rather, you look forward to the future with hopefulness. An example of a guilty thought is, "Okay, I made a mistake; so what am I going to do about it?"

Inappropriate guilt, when you feel guilty without cause, prolonged guilt after a change has been made, or guilt distorted to become an attack on your character or general worth are not productive and need to be resolved.

Shame

Shame is getting stuck and obsessing on a mistake, which often leads to doubt, discouragement, and questioning your character. This negative process most often perpetuates a cycle of failure and leads to feeling hopeless, which can defeat the desire to keep trying. A shameful thought is, "Only bad people make mistakes like this; I must be a bad person." It is very useful to distinguish between guilt and shame and ask yourself which one you are experiencing. See if you can catch yourself thinking thoughts that generate shame. Feeling guilty is okay and can actually help one to change. If you are experiencing shame, change your thoughts to focus on the bad behavior and remind yourself that you are not bad, even though your behavior might be labeled as "bad."

Toxic shame is another thing; it is not a feeling that you have done a bad thing, but that you are a bad person. Toxic shame is based on faulty core beliefs. A discussion of how to change those beliefs is in chapter nine of this book.

Overcoming Bad Habits

Use all of the Thought Shield techniques to better control unwanted thoughts and behaviors. This is especially true if a behavior has developed into a habit. Experience has taught me that just wishing a habit to go away will only set me up for more failure and discouragement. Habits go away kicking and screaming; they require lots of determination to overcome. When a client comes back after a Thought Shield session and tells me it wasn't much help, I often find that the client has left a step out. For example, by not doing something physically different. Or, they may have only used one of the Three S's. The power and effectiveness of the Thought Shield depends on following all the steps.

Understanding the Escalation Process

I would like to further illustrate escalation by introducing you to Clarence, who came to get help for a serious habit involving Internet pornography. When he first entered therapy he was viewing pornography about three nights per week, about two hours per night.

Before he came in, Clarence had tried everything he could think of to stop, but nothing seemed to work. In fact, in spite of his best efforts, he felt that the habit was getting worse. For example, he found himself erasing his pornography history for fear someone would stumble across it, he was becoming irritable with others when he couldn't find an acceptable excuse to get on the Internet for pornography, he was having more and more disturbing sexual fantasies, and he was isolating himself from family and friends so he could indulge in his habit. Clarence was engaged and planning on getting married in two months. He finally decided to disclose his problem to his fiancé, and they decided he should seek help.

Now, let's look at escalation step-by-step using Clarence as an example.

Step One:

First, Clarence identified a behavior he wanted to have more control over, (A) Internet pornography. As his pornography use increased in frequency, his amount of control had diminished. I suggested he use a tracking chart (B), to track the frequency of the behavior and determine where he was along the escalation scale.

I told Clarence, "At each level of escalation you make choices that will contribute to your feelings of control or lack of, such as the frequency of your Internet use (C). There is probably nothing that builds self-esteem more than taking back control of an unwanted behavior. It is liberating! This exercise will take some discipline, but the rewards will be well worth your efforts."

A. Behavior that you would like to have more control over:
Using the Internet to view pornography once a week.

B. Tracking Chart:

Sunday	Monday	Tuesday	Wednesday	Thursday	Friday	Saturday
	II				*III*	*II*

C. Choices

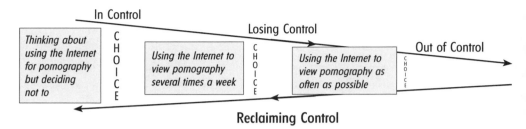

Step Two:

I explained to Clarence, "Once you have identified a behavior, tracked its frequency and identified some of the contributing choices, the second step in reclaiming control is to (A) set a goal and (B) identify the appropriate steps to take in accomplishing the goal. Writing your goal down will help you make the commitment to follow through. Commit to using the Thought Shield every time you struggle with an unwanted thought as you work to accomplish your goal. Remember, the earlier you apply the Thought Shield, the greater impact and control you will have on your choices!"

A. Goal for reclaiming control:

Example:

I will make a mindful decision to use the Internet only when someone else is present.

B. Steps to take in reclaiming control:

Example:

(1) I will keep the computer room door open at all times; (2) I will position my computer so I am facing the door; (3) I will never use the computer if I am alone (4) If I slip, I will tell my fiancé immediately.

Step Three:

I continued my instructions to Clarence, "Now that you have completed steps one and two, your next step will be to identify the thoughts, feelings, and behaviors that have established your movement through the escalation scale. Also note whether your behavior has become a habit or addiction. There is the possibility that as you have moved through the scale that you have bypassed a level of the scale, for example, you have jumped from having the *thought* of wanting to be on the Internet viewing pornography to being in the *habit* of being on the Internet for pornography. If this happens it is important that you are aware of it, and know how to avoid it."

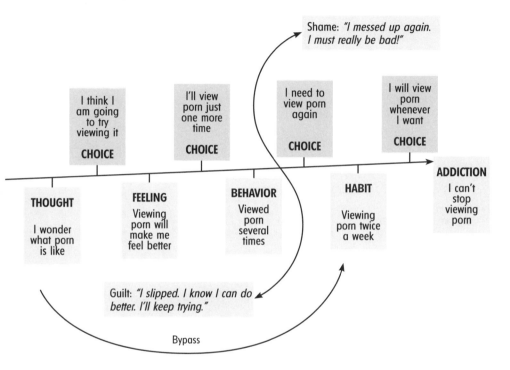

Step Four:

Finally, I explained to Clarence, "As you move through the escalation scale you may experience feelings of guilt and/or shame. While these feelings are common, they can cause undue stress. It is important that you be aware of these feelings and how they affect you. Guilt can be healthy and productive when you use it as a catalyst to do better. On the other hand, shame is destructive because it affects your core feelings of worth; shame should be avoided. As you learn to identify when you are feeling guilt compared to when you are feeling shame over your thoughts or behaviors, you will begin to hang onto your 100% worth even when you are struggling with your behaviors. In allowing yourself to utilize guilt as a catalyst to do better, you will feel better about yourself."

A.

Guilt: *When I give into my urge to view Internet pornography I feel as though I am weak and have let myself down, but I will do better tomorrow.*

_____

_____

Shame: *My constant Internet pornography viewing makes me feel ashamed and out of control; it feeds my habit so I feel worthless.*

_____

_____

B. Describe how you let feelings of guilt and/or shame affect you:

When I become aware of my feelings of guilt or shame, I begin to feel depressed. I also have a tendency to beat myself up emotionally; use the Internet to view porn even more.

Applying these steps to your own behavior

As you work through the Escalation Worksheet which follows, it is important to remember that the key to success in overcoming any unwanted behavior is learning to identify and label the preceding thoughts and feelings earlier. Learning to do so will diminish escalation and increase your ability to stay in control.

Control of your life begins by controlling the nature and quality of your thoughts. As you change your thinking, you will, over time, change your life. A wise mentor once told me that, "Whether you think you can, or can't, you are probably right." Control brings positive feelings about yourself, as well as a sense of well-being and balance. Few things create a stronger sense of self-confidence and self-esteem than taking control of your life. Even so, there are often powerful things that tend to get in the way of self-control: doubt, procrastination, minimizing, fear, and the potential negative impact of unresolved conflict. As you practice consistently identifying and labeling unwanted thoughts earlier, such as doubt and procrastination, their energy will decrease.

ESCALATION WORKSHEET

Directions

Step One: Identify a behavior in your life that you would like to have more control over. Track the frequency of this behavior by making a mark in the appropriate box each time the behavior occurs. At the end of the tracking period (7 days) tally up your total and decide where you are on the escalation scale. Then fill in a choice at each level in the scale below that you feel has contributed to your losing control (go only to the level where you are at). Start first with a simple behavior.

A. Behavior that you would like to have better control over:

_____

B. Tracking Chart

Sunday	Monday	Tuesday	Wednesday	Thursday	Friday	Saturday

C. Choices

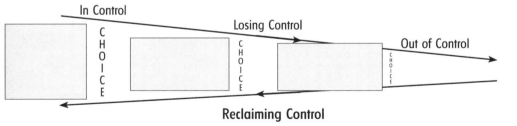

Step Two: Make a goal for reclaiming control over this particular behavior and record what steps you will need to take. (Include interventions such as the Thought Shield and mindfulness).

A. Goal for reclaiming control:

_____
_____
_____

B. Steps to take in reclaiming control:

_____
_____
_____

Step Three: Identify the thoughts, feelings, and behavior, and determine whether the behavior has become a habit or an addiction. Include the choices you made along the escalation scale. If it seems as though you have bypassed any of these, indicate by drawing an arrow from where you started to where you ended up (see the example).

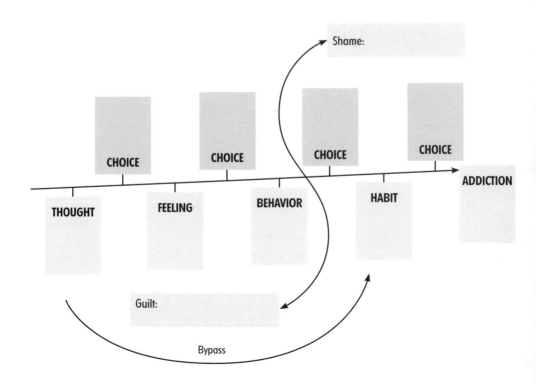

Step Four: Identify if you have feelings of guilt and/or shame. Record these feelings in the space provided. (Definitions of guilt and shame can be found on pg. 69).

Guilt: _____

_____

Shame: _____

_____

Describe how you let feelings of guilt and/or shame affect your behavior:

_____

_____

_____

_____

_____

Impartial and Benevolent Observer

The final tool in this chapter is learning to be an *impartial and benevolent observer.* This means you provide yourself with nurturing as well as a caring attitude as you stand back and view your life in an impartial way. Have you ever considered viewing yourself in the same impartial way you might view a friend?

When a close friend or loved one is having a hard time, feeling down, or beating himself up emotionally, what would you do? Would you offer help and support? After listening, you might provide comfort, encouraging your friend to be more hopeful. Among other things, you might remind him of the good things in his life. In a sense, you become his cheerleader. A true friend tries to be available to listen, encourage, and show love. Would you give up on your friend or would you try your best to be there for him?

You choose to be impartial by treating yourself as you would a friend in need, by being equally patient and caring. As you act benevolently towards yourself by developing a desire to do good towards yourself, you become the benefactor of your own good will.

For example, once you have stopped an unwanted thought long enough to apply mindfulness and used reframing, you could use the impartial and benevolent observer technique. Imagine looking at yourself with the idea of providing nurturance and a caring attitude towards yourself. You might imagine saying something to yourself like, "I'm proud of you for being mindful and stopping that thought. Now I want to encourage you to use the Thought Shield and then do something physically different. I know you can do it because I have seen you do it before!" And then, reinforce yourself for being successful by patting yourself on the back.

Using the impartial and benevolent observer tool is a whole new way of thinking and learning how to take care of you. Don't be discouraged if it takes a little practice. You may want to let a friend know what you are doing to change how you view yourself and ask for feedback and support.

I usually don't recommend using the impartial and benevolent observer tool until you have successfully solved a problem by using the Thought Shield, reframing, and stopping/starting. This is because the impartial and benevolent observer is an advanced tool that requires more mindfulness and usually does not come naturally. Once you have a good handle on using the other tools, it will be easier to begin using this tool.

Conclusion:

You have now learned how to use a very powerful set of tools for better control of thoughts and behaviors. Remember that taking back control of certain issues in your life can be challenging and will require you to be persistent. Don't give up; apply *all* the tools learned in this chapter. Even so, some problems might need the assistance of a professional counselor, so don't be afraid to ask for help if you seem unable to conquer an issue in your life by yourself. Next you will be introduced to the principle of self-esteem.

Thought Shield Reminders

Notes and Insights

7

Self-esteem

S elf-esteem is more a by-product of being true to your values and beliefs than it is something you can "create." When I talk about self-esteem I am not talking about self-obsession, self-absorption or egotism. I'm not talking about the good feelings a teenager gets when they are "popular." I'm talking about the feelings that naturally result when you invest your life's energies in choices that mirror your beliefs. If you say you are committed to your family, for example, that you treat them well and spend time with them. Similarly, you are likely to feel good about yourself, to "esteem" yourself when you are a person who can be trusted. The congruence and honesty that leads to good self-esteem contributes greatly to good mental and physical health.

How Self-Esteem is Different from Self-Worth

Your worth is a gift no one can ever change or take away from you and is the expression of you as a total being, your inward value. One way to imagine this idea is to think of self-worth as always being 100%. Self-esteem, on the other hand, is changeable; it goes up and down like a meter according to the conclusions you are making about yourself at the time. Your self-esteem mirrors your judgments, conclusions, thought distortions, interpretations, and how you choose to respond to all external and internal stimuli. Five factors influence your self-esteem meter, (1) your concept of self, (2) your concept of others, (3) your self-talk, (4) your behavior, and (5) your environment, especially the opinions of others and the feedback you get from them. Each of these five factors will be discussed in greater detail in the pages following.

An interesting relationship exists between your self-esteem and your self-worth; because your self-worth is a gift, it has inherent qualities that are unchangeable and can never be taken away. Every human being has *great* worth. So, you may think, if that is true, why do I feel like I am not worth much sometimes? When this happens, it is not your worth you are questioning, it is your esteem. Whenever your esteem is down, for whatever reason(s), you will be out of balance and at risk of thinking, saying, and doing things that are not healthy for the relationship you have with yourself and others. As you will see in the following figure (*Fig. 7.1*), although self-esteem and self-worth are related, they are also different in several important ways and it is important to understand the difference.

Factors that move your esteem meter up or down

We can look at the factors that move your self-esteem meter up or down. One way to visualize Concept of Self (CS = how I feel about me) and Concept of Others (CO = how I feel about others and how I believe they feel about me) is to think of two different people (such as a husband and wife, or two life-long best friends) who have enormous influence on each other even though they are independent of one another. When a close friend gives me a compliment, my esteem meter will go up. Similarly, if my close friend makes a negative comment towards me it is likely my meter will go down because of the respect I have and the influence that friend has on me. Our choices and behavior have reciprocal effects on those around us. This is *especially* true in close relationships. An angry comment from a loved one can be devastating and take a big toll on a relationship. Part of maturity is learning to rise above negative feedback from others—realizing it may have little to do with you, but be rooted in their own low self-esteem and other problems they are dealing with.

SELF-ESTEEM vs. SELF WORTH

SELF-ESTEEM METER
What I think/say/do

SELF-WORTH
Who I Am

I am really feeling on top of most things in my life. Most of my thoughts are positive.

Not much is going right in my life. I am confused about many things and having trouble making decisions. Most of my thoughts are negative.

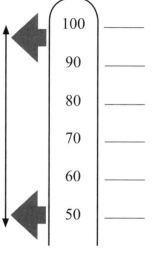

100
90
80
70
60
50

Your meter goes up and down according to these influence factors:
1. Your concept of SELF
2. Your concept of OTHERS
3. Your self-talk
4. Your behavior
5. Your environment

As you learn to gain control over those things that influence your self-esteem, you will experience the following benefits:
1. Personal BALANCE
2. UNITY in relationships
3. Peace and HARMONY with self and others
4. DURABILITY in relationships

* The self-esteem meter starts at "50" rather than "0" because I have never encountered a person who had absolutely no self-esteem (despite what he/she might have thought).

Fig. 7.1

Influence Factors One (CS) and Two (CO)

The three diagrams below (Fig. 7.2) show several different ways of relating to others in comparison to the relationship one has with him- or her-self.

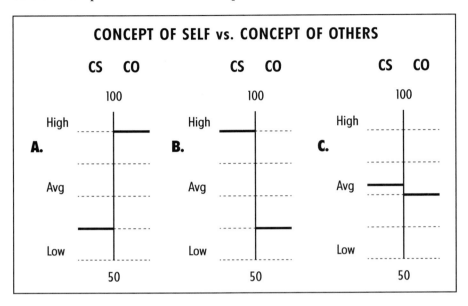

CONCEPT OF SELF vs. CONCEPT OF OTHERS

A. This configuration shows an overemphasis on others at the expense of self (and is out of balance). In other words, you are very worried about and put a lot of weight on what others think of you or what they will say about you. You will not listen to yourself even if you know the advice from others is not in your best interest. Everything is downhill to you in this way of relating to others. You are in trouble if the others you listen to are manipulative, having a bad day, are not well informed, do not have your best interest in mind, or are suffering from OBS themselves.

B. Configuration "B" is exactly the opposite of "A" in that you only think about what benefits you (and again, is out of balance). You could care less about what others think, say or do. Two major problems with this approach to life are that you are not teachable, and can be blind to advice that might benefit you greatly.

C. As you can see from this configuration, your emphasis on self-direction—paying more attention to what is going on inside than outside-- is generally just a little higher than your concern about others' opinions. However, you don't know everything and will often need to consult with others. Your openness to other's opinions will be a little higher than your emphasis on self for that experience. This healthy balance makes you teachable and flexible. The give and take means you can learn from your mistakes and take corrective action when needed.

On the next page you will find a worksheet designed to help you assess where you are on the self-esteem meter and determine where your concept of self versus concept of others is.

SELF-ESTEEM METER and CS/CO WORKSHEET

1. Mark on the self-esteem meter, where you feel your self-esteem is.

2. Refer to Figure 7.2. On the diagram below, draw a line representing where you think your concept of self (CS) and your concept of others (CO) are at this time in your life, putting CS on the left side and CO on the right.

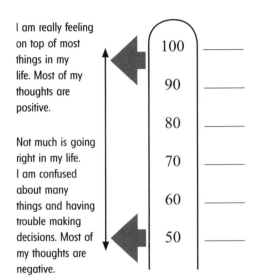

I am really feeling on top of most things in my life. Most of my thoughts are positive.

Not much is going right in my life. I am confused about many things and having trouble making decisions. Most of my thoughts are negative.

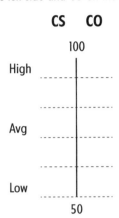

Write about what it would take to move your self-esteem meter up 4 or 5 points.

Example: *Identifying negative self-talk and practicing reframing it.*

a. _____
b. _____
c. _____
d. _____

Once you recognize movement, write down what you did to cause it.

Example: *I noticed that the more consistent I was at reframing, the better I felt and the more my self-esteem meter moved up.*

_____
_____

Why did you mark the self-esteem meter where you did?

_____
_____

Influence Factor Three (Self-Talk)

Your self-talk has a TREMENDOUS influence on your concept of self, concept of others, what you do, your quality of life and even your physical self. There are two types of thoughts: (1) Purposeful thoughts, those thoughts you purposefully put into your mind, such as planning what to say or do or when you purposefully, mindfully choose affirming thoughts. (2) Automatic or involuntary thoughts that just pop into your mind; you wonder where they came from. Some are positive, some are negative, and sometimes you might wonder how you could have ever had such a thought. Although you have no control over automatic thoughts popping into your mind, you do have control over what you do with those thoughts. If you choose to dwell on them your self-esteem meter can immediately go down. If you choose to substitute a positive mindful thought your self-esteem meter will go up.

If we dwell on automatic thoughts such as "That was really stupid," or "I sure must be dumb," we can start to believe we really are stupid or dumb. However, when a negative thought pops into your mind, you can learn to change it immediately by using the Thought Shield technique described in Chapter Six.

Influence Factor Four (Your Behavior)

Your behavior, what you actually do and say, also has an immediate impact on your self-esteem meter for positive or negative. For example, if you are doing things that push guilt buttons or that depresses you; your self-esteem meter will move down and make you feel Out of Balance. On the other hand, if you are doing and thinking that which is positive and affirming your self-esteem meter will always head upwards.

One of the most powerful and common enemies of self-esteem is being critical of yourself. Being self-critical is usually a product of earlier experiences with parents, siblings, friends, and your environment. It should be considered as an enemy; it is toxic. If your parental "cup" was abusive or critical with messages such as, "You are dumb," or "Can't you do anything right," you might still be hearing and struggling with this kind of negative self-talk from them.

Every time the critic inside attacks you, he is doing real psychological harm to you. He is inflicting wounds that will make it more difficult for you to feel you belong, that you can be productive, that you are competent. Use the Thought Shield technique to gain control and put a stop to the negative cycle. The critic hides in secrecy and darkness. Here are four ways to unmask and challenge him and put light on him:

1. Get to know your enemy by identifying his voice. What is his voice like? What are the words he uses to set you off?
2. Learn the physical symptoms that show you are under attack, such as becoming cross and irritable, depressed, or discouraged.
3. Become aware of his purpose. For example, is your inner critic getting you to avoid needed changes by escalating your fear of confrontation?
4. Call him out in the open, talk back to him, challenge him. Don't take him at face value.

Remember, the critic does not have your best interest at heart. You cannot afford what he does to you--the cost is too high.

An impressive article written by Jo Ann Larsen, DSW in the *Deseret News* entitled *Personal Credo for Enhancing Self-Esteem* (11 December 1988) included a list of self-esteem enhancing affirmations. I have altered her ideas slightly to better fit with the contents and flow of this chapter.

- I separate my worth from my behavior, as I have come to believe there is a difference between them. I can find ways to change and improve my behavior; however these changes have to do with me making choices that increase my integrity, and not my worth.
- I will make every effort to be in the present and not dwell on the mistakes of the past, remembering that my mistakes do no reflect on my worth. I acknowledge that I cannot grow unless I am willing to risk making mistakes in my efforts to change. I will notice and celebrate my efforts and successes along the way, whether big or small.
- I will remember that I am not perfect. When I receive disapproval from others, who are also imperfect, for something I have said or done, I will remind myself that I cannot control others – only how I will react.

- I will stop focusing on relationships where others don't have my best interests in mind and will instead focus on nurturing myself and my strengths. I will persistently release myself from negative labeling and will be more consistent in reframing such destructive self-talk.
- I recognize that I am unique in many positive ways and will stop comparing myself to others. I will develop and use the skill of becoming a more benevolent and impartial observer of myself; doing so will strengthen my decision-making so I am not bound by fear and indecisiveness. I will exercise my right to make my own decisions, taking into account suggestions from those I respect and trust.
- I will remind myself of the traits of a person who can be trusted and use those guidelines as I learn to trust myself and others.

Influencing Factor Five (Your Environment)

Environmental factors also influence your self-esteem meter positively or negatively. Some examples of environmental factors might be:

1. A home in which positive or negative is emphasized
2. Friends you associate with
3. Your school or job atmosphere

When I think about how the environment can influence us and how the choices we make can have a big influence on the environment, one way or the other, I'm reminded of a story about two frogs. These two frogs were exploring a farm yard on a cold rainy day when they came across a warm container. The farmer had just finished milking his cow and had left a bucket of warm milk sitting while he ran an errand.

The warm bucket felt so good as they pressed against it and was so enticing that the two frogs couldn't help but wonder what was inside. After all, if the outside was this good, what must the inside feel like? Curiosity overtook them and they both jumped in. Oh, the warm milk felt so good, as they had suspected, but it did require a certain amount of energy to stay afloat.

After a while they both began to tire. One frog said to the other, "I don't think I am going to be able to keep this up" and quit, sinking to the bottom. The other frog, instead of quitting, became more determined and with one last surge of energy, kicked his legs harder and faster. Shortly he noticed that the milk was beginning to thicken; soon it hardened, turning into butter, allowing him to plant his feet and jump out of the bucket.

The choices we make about how to respond to our environment greatly influence what happens to us. We can give in and be acted upon, taking whatever comes, or we can act and have a positive influence. We don't have to let the opinion, words, or even abuse of others damage our self-esteem. We can remember that the negative opinions and treatment of others do not affect our worth one iota.

You are getting closer to completing your personal balance "rope" (trust, boundaries in relationships, managing your energy, and self-control). You have learned that self-esteem affects all aspects of your life for positive or for negative. Review your self-esteem meter often, and think about the five influencing factors in your life. As you consistently put the self-esteem concepts to use, you will notice an enormous boost to your general sense of well-being. In Chapter Eight, you will be introduced to some very important thoughts for self-care.

Notes and Insights

8

Self-care

At the end of a week, have you ever caught yourself thinking, "The week is gone and I've been so busy I didn't have a minute for myself. Where did the time go?" Then, at the end of the next week, did you find yourself thinking the same thing? If you relate, be careful, this is a burnout waiting to happen.

If you let months slip by without adequate self-care you will suffer Out of Balance Syndrome because you are not taking care of the relationship you have with yourself. This usually happens because you OVERemphasize relationships you have with others, at the expense of self. (Go back and review Concept of Self and Concept of Others in Chapter 7).

Work in 3's

There are three major areas to consider in achieving personal balance for self-care. They are:

physical   social   emotional

Physical Self-Care

If you are like many people, you get up, plug in, run through the day to get things accomplished, then unplug and crash. The next day you repeat the same scenario. You are accomplishing a lot, but the way you are managing your time may not be in your best interest.

On the other hand, you may be a person who spends two or three hours a day working out at the gym or spa. You may be *very fit* as a result, but it may be at the expense of other important areas of your life. OVERemphasizing **any** area of your life results in OBS.

Some examples of healthy physical self-care might include:

- Getting to bed most nights at a decent time
- Eating three balanced meals a day
- Avoiding "junk food"
- Taking prescribed medications as directed
- Practicing deep relaxation with meditation
- Getting a massage
- Taking walks
- Hiking, bicycling, exercising
- Taking a nap when tired
- Developing your creative side

Benefits of consistently, mindfully practicing these activities include being more alert, creative, energetic, and living an overall more balanced, healthy and less stressful life. Following is a worksheet that will help you develop a healthy physical self-care plan.

PHYSICAL SELF-CARE WORKSHEET

Write down some examples of healthy physical self-care that are important to you:

_____

_____

_____

_____

_____

Write down physical self-care activities you are doing regularly:

_____

_____

_____

_____

_____

Write down physical self-care activities you are not currently doing that you believe would help you have better physical balance:

_____

_____

_____

_____

_____

_____

Be mindful of your physical needs. Make a plan to carry out the items listed in your physical self-care worksheet.
Be specific and make the commitment to follow through with your plan.

_____

_____

_____

_____

_____

Social Self-Care

How does a person achieve social balance? If you feel good only when you are in the company of others and can't stand being alone you may be neglecting your relationship with yourself. Most people need to avoid isolation, to get out and be social. However, others easily become over-stimulated with human contact and find it nerve-racking. Just getting out may not be enough in any case. Some people feel alone in a crowd; even though they have many contacts with people during the day, they may still feel lonely because they find it difficult to connect with others. Having good balance between your individual needs and your relationship needs depends not only on connecting with others but *how* you connect with them. You need to assess your own unique needs for meaningful social contact and find healthy ways to fill them.

Research indicates the benefits of not only having friends, but also having *close* friends. The Relationship Continuum on p. 34 in Chapter 4 shows how we move acquaintances up to the status of friends and friends to the status of close friends. The benefits of having close friends are many.

- Having a confidant with whom you can share anything, and who will still remain your close friend

  > Studies done over the last two decades involving more than 37,000 people show that social isolation – the sense that you have nobody with whom you can share your private feelings or have close contact with – doubles the chances of sickness or death.
  >
  > > House, J. et al. (1988). Medical risk of social relationships and health. *Science*. As cited in Goleman, D. (1997). *Emotional Intelligence*. Bantam Trade: New York, New York, p. 178.

- Decreasing feelings of depression

  > Among patients who felt they had strong emotional support from their spouse, family, or friends 54 percent survive heart transplants after two years, versus just 20 percent among those who reported little support. Similarly, elderly people

who suffer heart attacks, but have two or more people in their lives that they can rely on for emotional support, are more than twice as likely to survive longer than a year after an attack than those people with no support.

> Berkman, L. et al. (1992). "Emotional support and survival after myocardial infarction: A perspective population based study of the elderly." *Annals of Internal Medicin.* As cited in Goleman, D. (1997). *Emotional Intelligence.* Bantam Trade: New York, New York, p. 179.

- Less debilitating stress

    John Capioppo, an Ohio State University psychologist, did a roommate study of university students and concluded that, "It's the most important relation ships in your life, the people that see you day in and day out, that seem to be crucial for your health. And the more significant the relationship is in your life, the more it matters for your health."

    > Goleman, D. (1992, December 15). Interview for and article in *The New York Times.* As cited in Goleman, D. (1997). *Emotional Intelligence.* Bantam Trade: New York, New York, p. 179.

A study conducted by Suzanne Kobasa in 1984 determined that "stress is not the problem; it is our response to stress that largely determines whether we get sick or stay healthy. "The key to wellness", she determined, "is a different way of looking at and dealing with stressful events." She goes on to talk about "hardiness" as an important factor and discusses a term she calls "coherence." In part of her definition of coherence she states, "other research verifies that stress resistant personality traits include involvement in work or other tasks that have great meaning, the ability to relate well with others, and the ability to interact in a strong social network. The most vulnerable people are those who are socially isolated."

Kabasa, S.O. (1984, September). "How much stress can you survive?" *American Health*, pp. 71-72.

- Feeling that you belong

   A group of researchers went to Alameda County, California, and gathered data on more than 7,000 people over a nine-year period. At the end of the study, they found the common denominator that most often led to good health and long life: the amount of social support a person enjoys.

   Researchers who conducted the study concluded that people with social ties – regardless of their source – lived longer than people who were isolated. And people "who have a close-knit network of intimate personal ties with other people seem to be able to avoid disease, maintain higher levels of health, and in general, to deal more successfully with life's difficulties."

Padus, E. (1986). *The Complete Guide to Your Emotions and Your Health*. Emmaus, Pennsylvania: Rodale Press.

Set a goal to establish two close friends. The length of time it takes to do this isn't important; just set the goal and work towards accomplishing it. Look at your pool of acquaintances and pool of friends. Decide who you want to get to know better and apply mindfulness (review on p. 59) to make more *close* friends. Learning to connect deeply with a few special friends is critical to emotional and long-term health.

There are few things worse than to believe you do not belong or that you don't have enough friends. Cynthia is an example. When Cynthia came in to see me she was very sad and complained of not feeling connected with anyone. As I got to know Cynthia she had a great sense of humor and a very creative nature, but she was also shy and unsure of herself. Her self-esteem was way down and she was not physically active. She could only name a few acquaintances and could identify no friends or close friends.

I challenged her to think of people she would like to get to know better. She surprised herself and found there were actually quite a few people she had on her "acquaintance list" that fit that description. Her homework was to find ways to spend time with these people and to pick two people she could step up to a friend level. This was difficult for her, but with lots of encouragement she decided to ask one person to go to lunch with her. She was pleasantly surprised and encouraged when this person accepted; she found out that the person she asked had wanted to ask her to do something for some time. They hit it off and decided to do other things together. It wasn't long before her self-esteem was going up.

The following worksheet will help you focus on and develop specific goals for better social self-care and social balance.

SOCIAL SELF-CARE WORKSHEET

The following activities will help you achieve healthy social balance:

1. Work actively and mindfully to find and maintain two or three close friends. List them below.

    1. _____

    2. _____

    3. _____

2. Write down two things you can do to enhance/strengthen your relationship with those identified above.

Example: *Make sure I do something with _____ at least twice a month.*

Relationship: _____

Plan: _____

_____

Relationship: _____

Plan: _____

_____

3. To achieve balance, set aside time every week to be alone and take care of your relationship with yourself. No T.V., no phone, no computer. Use this time to relax and meditate (get into your creative side), to develop a hobby, interest, or talent. Find some things you have a passion for and do them. To facilitate setting aside time, fill in the activity on the appropriate day. Make sure you also fill in the time you plan to do this. Evaluate the effectiveness in the provided space at the end of each day.

	Sun.	Mon.	Tues.	Wed.	Thurs.	Fri.	Sat.
Indicate the activity and time							

Did you follow through? How did it affect you?						

4. Try this exercise for the next seven days. At the end of the week, go back and see how you have spent your time. The goal here is to find a good balance between meeting individual and relationship needs. Now, see where you need to bring better balance into your life and make a plan to do these things during the next week.

Day 1

Individual and Relationship Activities   **Plan to bring better balance**

_____   _____
_____   _____
_____   _____
_____   _____
_____   _____

Day 2

Individual and Relationship Activities   **Plan to bring better balance**

_____   _____
_____   _____
_____   _____
_____   _____

Day 3

Individual and Relationship Activities   **Plan to bring better balance**

_____   _____
_____   _____
_____   _____
_____   _____
_____   _____

Day 4

Individual and Relationship Activities

Plan to bring better balance

_____   _____

_____   _____

_____   _____

_____   _____

_____   _____

Day 5

Individual and Relationship Activities

Plan to bring better balance

_____   _____

_____   _____

_____   _____

_____   _____

_____   _____

Day 6

Individual and Relationship Activities

Plan to bring better balance

_____   _____

_____   _____

_____   _____

_____   _____

_____   _____

Day 7

Individual and Relationship Activities

Plan to bring better balance

_____   _____

_____   _____

_____   _____

_____   _____

_____   _____

Emotional Self-Care

The way we emote – the feelings we have and the way we express them – can either boost our immune system or weaken it. The connection between emotions and illness stems from how we interpret and cope with the emotions – and often from how we avoid feeling them.

> "Feelings themselves cause us less trouble than our efforts to protect ourselves from them. When we don't experience the pain of difficult events – when we don't feel our feelings – we are much more prone to develop physical symptoms."
>
> Grossbart, T.A. & Sherman C. (July/August 1988). Getting under your Skin. *New Age Journal*, pp. 22-34.

Take a minute now and ask yourself what you are feeling at this moment. Can you remember a feeling you experienced sometime today? Very often, when I ask a client to tell me what he/she is feeling, the common answer is "I don't know."

What is feeling? *Merriam Webster's Collegiate Dictionary* (Tenth Edition) describes feeling as "a subjective response to a person, thing or situation." Feeling denotes any partly mental, partly physical response marked by pleasure, pain, attraction, or repulsion. Emotion carries a strong implication of excitement or agitation, but, like feeling, encompasses both positive and negative responses.

Finish the sentence: Right now I am feeling _____.

a.	Happy	g.	Good
b.	Anxious	h.	Frustrated
c.	Sad	i.	Wonderful
d.	Elated	j.	Devastated
e.	Discouraged	k.	Sexy
f.	Worried	l.	Comfortable

Expressing your feelings instead of stifling them would be an example of healthy emotional self-care; taking time to have fun is another.

Being stuck in a rut of doing things the same way day in and day out can cause boredom and feeling down. Taking time to figure this out (mindfulness) and consequently doing something different can make an enormous shift for the positive in your emotional life and could help push your esteem meter up.

Learning to be assertive – acting in a decisive and self-confident manner – is another aspect of healthy emotional self-care. However, there are big differences between being aggressive, passive and assertive. Let's look at definitions and examples of these three concepts.

In *Fig. 8.1*. The definitions following F*ig. 8.1* explain why learning to be assertive is the healthiest approach to all relationships. Learning to be assertive, for example, will help push your self-esteem meter up because of the increase in self-confidence it produces. Being assertive also increases the level of trust in oneself.

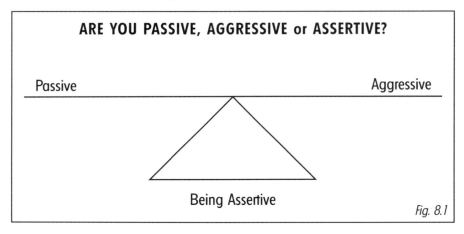

ARE YOU PASSIVE, AGGRESSIVE or ASSERTIVE?

Passive   Aggressive

Being Assertive

Fig. 8.1

Passive Approach to Relationships

Passiveness is being overly submissive, not standing up for yourself being lethargic when it comes to matters of importance, yielding to others at your expense. For example:

- Sitting back and being acted upon
- Not taking action when you really feel the need
- Taking the attitude it doesn't matter if you do or don't do something

Usually, the passive approach will cause you to feel weak and useless. Over time it will generate feelings of resentment towards yourself and others, a feeling of wanting to give up.

Aggressive Approach to Relationships

Aggressiveness is acting too intensely, being combative when interacting with others, and being too obtrusive for the situation. For example:

- Being constantly competitive, oppositional to whatever is said or done
- Being overly reactive, using too much negative energy
- Being forceful beyond reason
- Disregarding the rights or feelings of others

Being aggressive towards others drives them away. People will avoid you and/or want to get even with you. Neither passivity nor aggression are healthy approaches to relationships, and will tend to isolate you.

Assertive Approach to Relationships

Assertiveness is choosing to take a stand, to state positively what you are feeling and thinking without attacking the character of another. For example:

- Stating confidently what is on your mind without the need for proof of evidence
- Being teachable, and taking into account what others might suggest/ recommend, and making a decision and taking action
- Saying "Thank you" to a compliment
- Participating in an activity, even though you may feel a little uncomfortable

Expressing feelings forthrightly, but in a way that does not attack the character of others is enormously beneficial for building the self-confidence of yourself and others.

Being passive often results in feeling isolated, and being aggressive often causes others to avoid you. However, when you are assertive, you foster positive relationships. The next worksheet will assist you in identifying when you are being passive and/or aggressive. It will also help you in applying mindfulness, which enables you to be more assertive.

EMOTIONAL SELF-CARE WORKSHEET

1. Identify a situation in which you were either passive or aggressive.

Situation	(circle one)

Example:

*When my mother told me that I couldn't do anything
right, I just let her say it without defending myself, or*   (**passive**)   aggressive
telling her how it affects me.

A.

_____   passive   aggressive

B.

_____   passive   aggressive

C.

_____   passive   aggressive

2. Identify how you could have applied mindfulness (p. 59) to the situation in order
    to be assertive rather that passive or aggressive (remember mindfulness requires
    thinking differently and behaving differently).

Example: *I could have told her that such comments make me feel of little worth
and then reframed the situation by reminding myself that I do a lot
of things well—specifically, I bake really well and others are always
complimenting my baked goods.*

Situation A:

Situation B: _____

_____

_____

_____

Situation C: _____

_____

_____

_____

Adding Fun to Your Life

In light of the fact that so many of us tend to be too serious and critical, it is especially important to add fun to your life. Obviously, what is fun for one person may be boring to another. And, what may be fun to do for a while, may eventually become boring or feel like a task. With this in mind it is wise to pinpoint a variety of activities that are enjoyable and interesting enough that you would look forward to doing them. A major point here is learning to take time for fun and then following through, even if it means putting other things off. Remember to develop a balance between fun for yourself, fun with your spouse or significant other, and fun with your family, and, when time permits, fun with friends outside your family.

When I bring up the subject of fun I often get the response, "I just don't have time." Most of us don't *have* time for fun in busy schedules, and that's the reason so many of us suffer from OBS. For self-care to be a priority in your life you have to *make* it happen, you have to *take* time for fun. Otherwise, it will not happen enough to be beneficial.

Self-care is not a *selfish* pursuit, but rather a balanced approach between individual needs and relationship needs. So, don't forget to have fun often enough that it becomes a way of life, the same way that work does.

It is important to have fun developing talents, interests, and hobbies. Doing so will balance out the routine of work and other things that are demanded of you. A caution – write down the fun activity you plan to do and when you will do it. It helps to put it in your personal planner and on your calendar at home.

Otherwise, you run the risk of other demands taking its place. Remember that all work and no play, makes a pretty dull day!

Balance is vital in managing your fun time, just as balance is vital in all areas. Some years ago, while working as a supervisor of social services at the State Prison, I noticed a group of inmates moving up the corridor. A large, muscular man was in the middle of the group. As they passed, I noticed that his right arm stuck nearly straight out from his shoulder instead of hanging down to his side. The arm was enormous! I asked the warden about this man's arm. The warden said that the man was the arm wrestling champion of the prison. All he did all day long was lift weights with his right arm and take on anyone who would challenge him to an arm wrestling contest. How sad this was and how out of balance this man's life was.

Self-care often gets set aside because of the false belief that to care for one's self is bad, prideful, or selfish. We live in a very task-oriented society and as a result, you might be tempted to put this principle aside for a later time, or not use some of the ideas presented. But as you apply the principles of relationships in your life, your rope will grow in strength; all of the principles of relationships work together to create a holistic program for personal balance.

Conclusion

In Chapter Nine, you will read personal accounts of people who have used the principles for achieving personal balance and how they have benefited from their use. You will also have the opportunity to look back on each of the principles and assess your progress as you work on your own "principles of relationships rope."

Notes and Insights

9

Looking Back at the Six Principles for Achieving Personal Balance

O ne strand of sewing thread is easy to break. Try it yourself. Now, try two threads and you will notice they are still fairly easy to break. However, if you take three sewing threads and twist them together as if you were making a rope, you will find it is ten times more challenging to break them. Six threads twisted together can be almost impossible to break.

If you liken the threads to the Six Principles for Achieving Personal Balance discussed in this book, you can see that even though each principle is important, one alone lacks the strength and durability of all six principles combined. As you find more balance by incorporating all six principles into your life you will notice an enormous increase in your sense of well-being. Your self-esteem meter will be up and will fluctuate less. You will also feel more consistency and direction in your life.

Here is what the six principles look like when they are woven into a "rope" to create individual balance, strength, and durability.

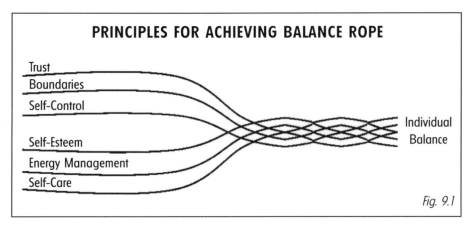

PRINCIPLES FOR ACHIEVING BALANCE ROPE

Trust
Boundaries
Self-Control

Self-Esteem
Energy Management
Self-Care

Individual
Balance

Fig. 9.1

Forming Your Rope

Now that you have been introduced to all six principles (strands of your rope) for achieving personal balance, how do you apply them--or symbolically make a rope out of them? Each principle is important, but only when you mindfully use all the strands together can you form a powerful rope to achieve personal balance.

If you were making a rope that you wanted to be strong enough to safely hold your weight, the first component you would want to consider is *trust*. You want to be able to depend on it! To develop trust in your rope you must practice each principle in your every-day life – there are no short cuts. You will develop trust in the principles as each strand of your rope becomes a trusted, tried and true friend. Each strand has its own purpose and functions independent of the other strands. Just as personal and relationship boundaries need to be established, *boundaries* need to be established between each strand of the rope, allowing for growth, understanding and independence. The key to forming

TESTIMONIAL

The ideas shared in *Six Principles for Achieving Personal Balance* have been a tremendous help to me in learning how to attain better equilibrium in my life. Jim taught me how to find what my individual needs were and maintain them in healthy ways. He also taught me how to become more self-confident, which allowed me to take more control of my life by focusing on three of his principles: self-control, self-esteem, and self-care. I have been able to resolve some issues that have plagued me my entire life by understanding how out of balance my life was and discovering how to manage my internal conflicts.

One of the areas I found most helpful was in understanding how to overcome obsessive behavior and the conflicts it brought into my life. Resolving this conflict has allowed me to look at life differently, reduce stress, think more clearly, given me more energy and improved important personal relationships. I learned that there are many things I cannot control, that appearing "perfect" takes more energy than it's worth, and that I *can* change old habits.

The concept of the Thought Shield is one of the most valuable concepts I learned. Jim's principle of "mindfulness" was eye-opening for me and liberated me from the inability to control my thoughts. The visual image of a stop sign was very effective in helping me learn to make the right choices to overcome self-destructive habits that had been issues for me most of my life. I have learned how to purposefully make better choices and that control of my life is dependent on the nature and quality of my thoughts.

Another revealing concept for me is that my self-worth is always 100%. I learned the importance of not comparing myself to others, but to compare me only to myself. Jim also showed me how to take care of myself and balance the physical, social and emotional aspects of my life. He helped me realize that I was out of balance with my social relationships and showed me how important close-knit personal relationships are in achieving good health and dealing more successfully with difficulties in life. I have become more confident in areas where I felt weak and I really feel that I have a much better approach to life and my relationships with others.

My association with Jim and being taught these principles has led me to an overall more healthy and less stressful life. I understand myself in new terms and have truly been able to reduce stress, improve my self-esteem, be more confident with the person I am and accept me for the great talents I have and the contributions I make. I am confident that you will also be able to make positive changes in your life by adopting the ideas taught in *Six Principles for Achieving Personal Balance*.

Loren C.

these boundaries is learning which principle(s) to use and when. This learning comes with consistent practice.

Control is another important issue in finding balance in your life.

Managing your energy is also a vital part of daily life. There is nothing more rewarding than feeling more energetic and positive about life. On the other hand, it is discouraging and costly to focus your time and energy on behaviors that you have little influence or control over. Learning to identify that problem and change your focus conserves energy, and is much healthier. If you focus too much on one aspect of your life or on one principle, that particular strand weakens due to overuse.

Because you will always want to keep your rope in good repair, it is important to maintain all six principles—giving them the upkeep they need. You do this by regular study of how to apply the principles in different situations in your life. The majority of us forget that finding time to relax, meditate, and have fun are included in self-care and are essential to keep your rope in good repair.

Here's another analogy for the Six Principles of Personal Balance: Imagine an old-fashioned stagecoach with six horses pulling it. The coach is carrying a priceless load of gold. Each horse has its own, separate rein. The horses have been hand picked and then teamed up because they pull together well as a team. A skilled coach driver learns each horse's temperaments, strengths and weaknesses. For example, one horse might want to work too hard and need prompting to slow down and relax from time to time. When one horse is having a bad day the driver will encourage the other horses to pick up the slack because he wants to deliver the precious cargo safely.

You can use this analogy as you practice and become consistent in using the principles. Each principle or strand is like an individual horse. Each has its own strengths, but when "pulling together" they are much stronger. You are like the coach driver, and as you practice taking control of using these six principles in your life, you see how well they work together as a team.

We will now look at how beliefs play an important part in the six principles you have been learning about.

Review of Core Beliefs

A belief is any established and consistent pattern of thinking. Beliefs formed in one's youth are generally firmed up by adolescence and are strong and persistent. A faulty core belief is a very strong, imbedded *negative* belief that greatly influences how one thinks and behaves.

Faulty core beliefs (FCB) are formed as a result of life experiences that are consistently unhappy. They tend to make a person question their self-worth. A common doubting thought that can lead to a faulty core belief is: "Maybe I am a bad person." Dwelling on a negative, doubting thought about one's character is the seedbed for developing a FCB. When a belief such as "I am a bad person" becomes established it is hard to repair. The repair process will be described in the following pages.

Repairing faulty core beliefs is not an easy task, but can be done. Everyone has the capacity to modify – through conscious, rational choice – their beliefs and perceptions regarding their self-concept. We *can* choose who we want to be and in turn can change belief systems by making new choices, taking new actions and experimenting with new responses. Sometimes a professional (usually a counselor) will be needed to help repair persistent, negative thinking. Let's discuss this repair process.

Faulty Core Belief Repair Process

Although repairing FCBs can be a daunting task, with the right tools and hard work you can do it! To help you visualize the process, I have provided two figures. *Fig. 9.2* shows the entire process of how a faulty core belief is developed and repaired. Following a general description of the process, *Fig. 9.3* illustrates the process using a specific example. Let's begin with number one in *Fig. 9.2*.

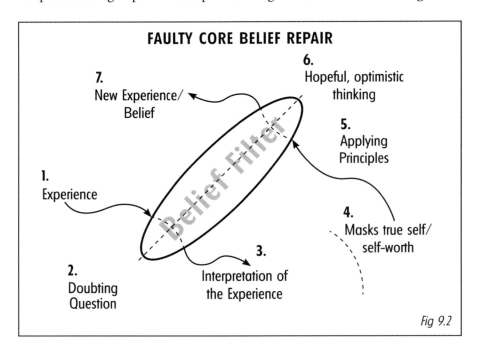

FAULTY CORE BELIEF REPAIR

7. New Experience/ Belief

6. Hopeful, optimistic thinking

5. Applying Principles

1. Experience

Belief Filter

4. Masks true self/ self-worth

2. Doubting Question

3. Interpretation of the Experience

Fig 9.2

1. The first step in repairing a FCB is identifying life experiences that have been *unhappy* and *ongoing*.
2. The ongoing, unhappy experiences cause questions and doubt to arise about one's character and worth. These questions and doubts, as they pass through your belief filter, form your FCB.
3. The output of the belief filter is the interpretation that the ongoing negative experiences indicate the person's true self, and a faulty core belief (FCB) is established.
4. The FCB masks the person's true identity and worth. It could be a FCB that one is inadequate, not lovable, or hopeless. What makes this type of thinking/feeling faulty is the fact (from this author's perspective) that

everyone is always *worth* 100%. A person's self-esteem, on the other hand, can fluctuate based on one's interpretation of life experiences (see Principle Four), and can be impacted positively by the five influencing factors and the other principles for personal balance.

5. Challenging the established FCB can be a demanding task, but by using the principles and the corresponding tools that apply (i.e. self-control, mindfulness, the Thought Shield, reframing, etc.), a person can begin to repair his/her FCB.

6. By consistently using the principles, one begins to weaken and change the FCB, passing it back through the belief filter. Now, instead of a negative, doubting question about who you are as a person, a new, hopeful and encouraging belief starts to develop. Remember, the key here is consistently challenging the FBC with the principles for achieving personal balance.

7. As the FCB passes back through the belief filter, a new, healthy core belief begins to emerge and develop. Please don't be discouraged in this process. FCBs can be persistent because they have been in your mind for a long time. With consistent effort you can convince yourself that your FCB is no longer a part of your life.

Now, we will see how all this applies by looking at an example of how a FCB can be repaired. This example will follow Jason's process in developing a FCB, as well as the process he followed to repair the FCB.

1. Jason came to believe that his father has rejected him, as evidenced by the following ongoing negative experiences:

   a. His father spent very little time with him.
   b. Jason felt that his father ignores him when others were present.
   c. His father frequently chose to go out with his friends, even after he had promised to go with him instead.

2. Because these disappointing experiences happened regularly, Jason could not excuse them to accident. His resulting feelings of low self-esteem and self-doubt led to the nagging thought, "Maybe I am worthless."

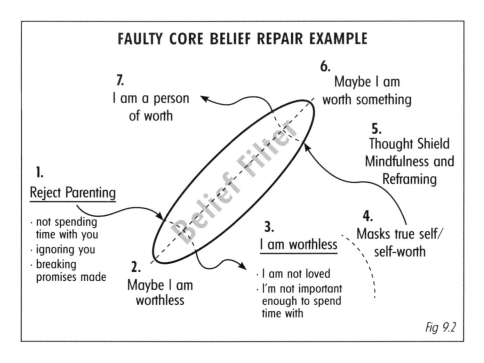

FAULTY CORE BELIEF REPAIR EXAMPLE

7.
I am a person
of worth

6.
Maybe I am
worth something

5.
Thought Shield
Mindfulness and
Reframing

1.
Reject Parenting

· not spending
  time with you
· ignoring you
· breaking
  promises made

Belief Filter

2.
Maybe I am
worthless

3.
I am worthless

· I am not loved
· I'm not important
  enough to spend
  time with

4.
Masks true self/
self-worth

Fig 9.2

3. After dwelling upon these negative experiences over a long period of time Jason developed the FCB, I am worthless." The justification for this belief was reinforced by thoughts such as:

    a. I'm not worth spending time with.
    b. I must be worthless because my father consistently ignores me.
    c. I am not loved.

4. This FCB masked Jason's self-worth, because ongoing experiences tend to validate his feelings of worthlessness.

5. In order to weaken and defeat this FCB, Jason must challenge it. The Thought Shield is an effective tool to stop the thought process every time the FCB occurs. It allows Jason to become mindful of how damaging the false belief truly is and that the price he pays is too high to continue dwelling on it. At this point Jason could use reframing, by thinking: "I know my father didn't spend much time with me, but I have several friends who value me enough to do fun things with me,"

or, "It seems like my sister and brothers value me because they come to all my school plays." Using such self-talk consistently to challenge the FCB, will over time, begin to weaken the FCB, which will begin to enable Jason to question the FCB with healthier thoughts.

6. This new thinking can begin to replace Jason's FCB with thoughts like, "Maybe I am worth something," instead of "Maybe I am worthless." This in turn will bring hopefulness and the possibility his thinking will change.

7. With consistency, Jason's FCB can be weakened and defeated, transitioning again, from "Maybe I am worth something," into, "I *am* a person of worth."

Two worksheets have been included to help you apply what you have learned as you have worked through the Six Principles of Personal Balance. The first worksheet will help you identify a FCB in your life, how it developed, and how to repair it. You will be using the process just learned in this chapter, but will also be asked to identify concepts from the six principles that can help you in the repair process.

The second worksheet will ask you to go back to chapter one to look at the FCB you identified there and to now apply the six principles for achieving personal balance to repair that belief. Using the two worksheets will be a final application for you to see how the six principles can indeed make a difference in your life in very direct ways.

FAULTY CORE BELIEF REPAIR WORKSHEET

List a faulty core belief that developed in your life as a result of ongoing negative experiences:

Example: *I felt rejected by my father.*

_____

_____

Make a list of the experiences that supported this faulty core belief:

Examples: 1.   *My father didn't spend time with me.*

2.   *I was often ignored by my father.*

3.   *On many occasions he broke promises to do things with me.*

1.   _____

2.   _____

3.   _____

What belief about yourself developed as result of the above experiences:

Example: I *started to think that maybe I was worthless*

_____

_____

Note: If you consistently have unhappy experiences, it is likely that your belief filter might begin interpreting these experiences as "I am worthless."

How did you eventually interpret these experiences:

Examples: 1.   *I'm not worth spending time with.*

2.   *I must be worthless because I'm ignored.*

3.   *I'm not loved.*

1.   _____

2.   _____

3.   _____

What principles did you use to challenge your faulty core belief?

Examples: 1.   *Self-control (Thought Shield, mindfulness, reframing)*

2.   *Self-esteem*

3.   *Boundaries.*

1.   _____

2.   _____

3.   _____

This is a good time to review the chapter on self-esteem.

After doing so, make a list of your strengths (the things you value about yourself). Don't be too analytical; just write things down as they come to you. Things such as your friendly nature, being on time, helping others are examples of things you could include in a list like this.

Strengths/values:

_____

_____

_____

_____

You will need to challenge the faulty core belief in order to change it. In order to act differently, you must think differently (mindfulness). You can use your list of strengths/values to help challenge the faulty core belief.

TESTIMONIAL

Because I have tried to live a life of good principles, because I have always tried to treat others kindly, I assumed I was doing all that I could to be happy. I frequently thought, "I am doing all that I can, so why am I feeling so sad?"

After meeting with Jim and after learning and putting into practice the principles he taught me, I am on my way to a truly healthy life.

I have read several self-help books in the past, but the healing ends as soon as I set the book down. Where these books have fallen short is focusing mainly on "self-help," and not much else. Jim offers a complete package, touching on all areas of concern.

For example, no one else has explained trust, the meaning of trust, what characteristics not to trust and the essential need for trust in our lives. I trusted no one. I was even holding back with my husband, whom I love dearly. I thought I could survive alone.

I've always had a great sense of my own worth, but I wondered why I let people take advantage of me. I was confusing self-worth for self-esteem. The self versus others meter was highly effective in teaching me that I had to be assertive, so that others would respect me and I could respect myself.

I've grown into the habit of managing, or over-managing, my time to the point that I am never finished. I can't accomplish enough, and I didn't allow myself time to rest or have fun. I'm ready to let go of the "I'm perfect" security blanket, and trade it in for a hammock, to be enjoyed regularly.

Living a life of rigid rules lulled me into thinking I had extraordinary self-control. In reality my thoughts have run wild and the inner critic in my head was brutally unkind to me. The alligators in my past were eating me alive and I didn't even know I was feeding them. I had accepted negative thought patterns as the way things were--things I couldn't change. The Thought Shield and the mindfulness concepts are powerful visually and mentally in overcoming unwanted thoughts in my head.

Growing up in a climate of abuse, I was taught to trust no one. How could I? Ironically, being abused also broke down all of my personal boundaries. I didn't know how to stop people from hurting me physically and emotionally.

Jim explained personal boundaries to me in such a way that I know how to protect myself. I recognize and acknowledge my own feelings. I act upon urges of self-preservation without hesitation. And I'm not angry anymore.

I will always use the principles taught me. I will need them to help me on my journey, like a flashlight, compass and sleeping bag. I know now I could not survive without self-esteem, friendship and trust. These are the gifts Jim has given me.

Julia R.

Think about this. Now that you have the six principles, how will you utilize them to improve your personal balance? I would like to give you a personal challenge and promise: use the principles daily to strengthen your concept of self and you will have better relationships with others.

This next worksheet brings the principles full-circle for you. When you started reading this book you had no idea what the six principles were, let alone what they could do for you. Even so, you identified a core issue in your life. Now, you will have the opportunity to use all the principles that apply to the issue you identified in Chapter One.

Keep in mind that you are a beginner with the principles, so be patient with yourself. Build your skills with practice. Even if you aren't where you would like to be with whatever issue you have identified, you are on your way simply because you identified an issue in your life.

FAULTY CORE BELIEFS EVALUATION and CHANGE WORKSHEET

Refer back to the experience you identified in Chapter One. Restate it below and evaluate where you are with it now that you have all six principles in your rope.

Faulty Core Belief: _____

Evaluation: _____

_____

_____

List principles for Personal Balance that you believe can act as "change agents" for your faulty core belief (mindfulness, Thought Shield, stopping/starting, reframing, managing energy, etc.).

_____
_____
_____
_____
_____

Make a plan for applying those change agents (be specific).

_____
_____
_____
_____
_____
_____

After applying the personal balance strategies listed above for two weeks, note below how your core belief is changing.

_____
_____
_____
_____

Final Thoughts

You have now completed the *Six Principles for Achieving Personal Balance* Congratulations! You have taken an important step in constructing the most important relationship in your life – the one you have with yourself. Although you have finished reading the six principles, you are just beginning the construction of a strong, durable rope. To further develop and maintain a strong personal balance, you will need to continue applying the six principles in your every-day life. To reinforce and master the principles, I encourage you to reread them often, making them an integral part of your life.

Be hopeful and confident that you can succeed in whatever you decide to do in life. Persistence builds and reinforces hope! Also, take time to develop gratitude. I have heard it said the healthiest emotion you can experience is gratitude. If you want to stay healthy and have less stress in your life, develop a habitual "attitude of gratitude." Regularly recognizing the good things you do as well as recognizing the good in others is an integral part of becoming and remaining happy and healthy.

One last note: apply mindfulness to every aspect of your life. Napoleon Hill said the most practical of all methods of controlling the mind is the habit of keeping it busy with definite purpose, backed by a definite plan. (Williams, P. and Thomas, Lloyd J. [2005]. *Total life coaching: A compendium of resources.* New York, NY: W. W. Norton, 110). The six principles can and will make a positive difference in your life.

Glancing Forward

The next book in this series is titled *Six Principles for Achieving Marital Harmony.* Its purpose is to teach couples how to develop balance in their relationship. In a day and age where there are so many distractions and outright attacks against the marital relationship, it is crucial to have specific tools to help you counter the opposition.

You will be given specific and helpful tools that will bring peace and fun to your marriage. *Six Principles for Achieving Personal Balance* discusses establishing and maintaining personal balance; *Six Principles for Achieving Marital Harmony* will help you do the same thing in your marital relationship. You will learn how to communicate, not just talk. You will learn how to get through the most difficult problems with the least amount of difficulty. You will learn the role values play in a healthy relationship, and much, much more.

I wish you the very best in life. You can contact me for further information at:*jimlewis@guidingpath.biz*, or visit the Guiding Path webpage at: *www. guidingpath.biz.*

Sincerely,

James B. Lewis, LCSW, CSAT